RECASTING
THE PAST

The goals of Boynton/Cook's Young Adult Literature series are twofold: to present new perspectives on young adult literature and its importance to the English language arts curriculum and to offer provocative discussions of issues and ideas that transcend the world of the adolescent to encompass universal concerns about the search for identity, security, and a place in life. The contributing authors are leading teachers and scholars who have worked extensively with adolescents and are well read in the genre. Each book is unique in focus and style; together, they are an invaluable resource for anyone who reads, teaches, and/or studies young adult literature.

Titles in the series

A Complete Guide to Young Adult Literature: Over 1,000 Critiques and Synopses from The ALAN Review, edited by Virginia R. Monseau and Gary M. Salvner (available on CD-ROM)

Conflict and Connection: The Psychology of Young Adult Literature, by Sharon A. Stringer

Heirs to Shakespeare: Reinventing the Bard in Young Adult Literature, by Megan Lynn Isaac

Interpreting Young Adult Literature: Literary Theory in the Secondary Classroom, by John Noell Moore

Reading Their World: The Young Adult Novel in the Classroom, edited by Virginia R. Monseau and Gary M. Salvner

Recasting the Past: The Middle Ages in Young Adult Literature, by Rebecca Barnhouse

Reel Conversations: Reading Films with Young Adults, by Alan B. Teasley and Ann Wilder

Responding to Young Adult Literature, by Virginia R. Monseau

Young Adult Literature: The Heart of the Middle School Curriculum, by Lois Thomas Stover

ECASTING THE PAST

THE
MIDDLE AGES
IN
YOUNG ADULT
LITERATURE

REBECCA BARNHOUSE

BOYNTON/COOK PUBLISHERS
HEINEMANN
PORTSMOUTH, NH

Boynton/Cook Publishers
A subsidiary of Reed Elsevier Inc.
361 Hanover Street
Portsmouth, NH 03801-3912
www.boyntoncook.com

Offices and agents throughout the world

Cataloging in Publication data on file at the Library of Congress.

ISBN: 0-86709-470-2

Editor: Lisa Luedeke
Production coordinator: Renee LeVerrier
Production service: Colophon
Cover design: Darci Mehall, Aureo Design
Manufacturing: Louise Richardson

Printed in the *United States* of America on acid-free paper
04   03   02   01   00   DA   1   2   3   4   5

Contents

Acknowledgments

I wish to thank Youngstown State University for awarding me an academic quarter of research leave to write this book, and *The ALAN Review* and *The Lion and the Unicorn* for permission to reprint material that originally appeared in their pages. Virginia Monseau's generosity is legendary and I am grateful to have benefited from it. My thanks also to Cynthia Brincat, Megan Isaac, and Isaiah Mackler for their thoughtful comments. Without the humor, encouragement, and editorial skill of Sid Brown this book would not have been written—my gratitude. And finally, my thanks to my parents, to whom I dedicate this book.

Introduction

Being True to the Past

Writers of fiction for adolescents have long mined the Middle Ages for settings and materials. Newbery Medal winners have included several novels with medieval settings: Eric Kelly's *The Trumpeter of Krakow* (1928), Elizabeth Janet Gray's *Adam of the Road* (1942), Marguerite de Angeli's *The Door in the Wall* (1949), as well as, more recently, Karen Cushman's *The Midwife's Apprentice* (1995). Many writers use their material responsibly, accurately portraying the medieval period. Others, however, allow their own moral sense to take precedence over historical accuracy. In so doing, they often perpetuate anachronistic fallacies, allowing modern attitudes about such topics as literacy and tolerance for diversity to pervade their presentation of the Middle Ages. As A.S. MacLeod writes in *Horn Book Magazine,* "Too much historical fiction for children is stepping around large slabs of known reality to tell pleasant but historically doubtful stories. Even highly respected authors snip away the less attractive pieces of the past to make their narratives meet current social and political preferences" (1998, 27). Katherine Paterson echoes this view from the novelist's perspective, in Celia Keenan's paraphrase: "being true to the past means being true to a time when moral and social sensibilities were different from today's. . . . [T]o sanitize the past is to do an injustice to it and to condescend to the present" (Keenan 1997, 370).

Since S. E. Hinton declared them to be so, young adult protagonists have frequently been outsiders who question the status quo. But young adult literature set in the Middle Ages gives its writers a particular challenge: If characters reject the values of their time, they should not do so by embracing current values. Novelists must strive to avoid implicitly condemning the entire medieval period for not being modern. They do condemn it when they show their main characters being distrusted by their contemporaries for being literate or clean or having anachronistically modern values. To an unlikely degree, novels set in the Middle Ages feature characters who yearn to read or write. Many of them want to become healers, and several display an admirable yet inaccurate tolerance for diversity. Writers must tread carefully in their portrayal not only of these characters, but of other characters' reactions to them, to avoid unintentionally condescending to the past, subtly stereotyping medieval people as ignorant, dirty, and suspicious of new ideas by their rejection of the protagonists, who are sometimes uncomfortably like modern teenagers.

The best historical fiction tells a good story and at the same time represents the past responsibly and accurately. Its writers check their didactic tendencies, and create memorable, sympathetic characters who may question some of the values and perceptions of their own eras, yet who are clearly shaped by those values. These characters act and react in ways that are fitting for their own time and place, not for modern America. Novelists must not only get the facts right, they must also present *all* of their characters as authentically medieval, reacting to people and events around them with authentically medieval sensibilities.

But how are teachers and librarians to judge historical accuracy, particularly when a book's setting is a time or place they don't know much about? Often they must rely on short book reviews, jacket blurbs, and novelists' reputations. Even if they did have time to read all the novels they passed on to students, it would be hard for them to assess the authenticity of many of them without taking a crash course in the historical period. That's where this book steps in to help: both as a crash course in the Middle Ages and as a guide to some of the fiction set there.

What's Velveeta Cheese Got to Do with It?

Amongst medievalists, there's a favorite phrase: "The Velveeta Cheese Theory of the Middle Ages." According to the theory, the Middle Ages are exactly the same, no matter where you slice them.

But of course, the European medieval era is anything but all the same. After all, it covers approximately a millennium, from about 500 to about 1500. During this time period, there were vast differences in languages, in art, in social systems, in what people ate and what they wore. Only looking at the period from a distance does it all seem the same, just as looking at earth from space might make you think it was all ocean.

Many of our stereotypes about the medieval period come from the Victorian era, which idealized and romanticized the Middle Ages—think of pre-Raphaelite paintings of Arthur's knights questing for the Holy Grail, for example. On the other side, and blame Renaissance writers for this notion, is the stereotype of the Middle Ages as a millennium of appalling ignorance and brutality. Were the Middle Ages really as gloomy as the phrase "the Dark Ages" implies? No. Were they barbaric? Yes, but no more barbaric than any era of human existence. Michael Clanchy points out that the "crusaders' atrocities in Jerusalem in 1099 were limited in scope, and perhaps also in intention, compared with Auschwitz" (1997, 17).

Certainly, there were dark points. The Vikings marauded England several times during the eighth and ninth centuries, sacking churches and villages, killing kings, priests, and commoners. By the time King Alfred the Great finally subdued the Vikings, the state of learning "had declined so thoroughly in England that there were very few men on this side of the Humber [River] who could understand their divine services in English, or even translate a single letter from Latin into English," as Alfred himself writes in his famous preface to his translation (from Latin into Old English) of Gregory the Great's *Pastoral Care* (Keynes and Lapidge 1983, 125). In response to this decline in learning, the king instituted a program to translate the books "most necessary for all men to know" (126) into Old English so that Christian learning wouldn't be lost entirely.

Contrast with this, however, the intellectual ferment of Charlemagne's court a century earlier, where a number of influential scholars were involved in "educational and religious reforms" as well as in composing sophisticated Latin verse and prose (Brown 1998, 14). Or the numbers of English and European scholars working in Spain in the eleventh and twelfth centuries to translate Greek works like Aristotle's *Ethics* from Arabic into Latin (they had been preserved by being translated from Greek into Arabic). Or the learning and the intellectual debates at the great universities in the twelfth and thirteenth centuries: The famous philosophers and theologians Thomas Aquinas, Albertus Magnus, Meister Eckhart, and Duns Scotus all taught at the University of Paris during the same twenty-year period, from 1240–1260. Darkness this is surely not. Throughout the medieval millennium, as with any period in history, there were towering peaks as well as shadowy valleys.

The medieval era is often divided into three parts: the Early, High, and Late Middle Ages. Other terms also indicate the differences between time periods and geographical areas. For example, in the Early Middle Ages we hear of the Carolingians, who lived in the geographical area that is now mostly France, and that was ruled by Charlemagne, his predecessors, and his successors in the eighth and ninth centuries. "Anglo-Saxon" refers to England from approximately 600–1100. Unlike the word "Carolingian," "Anglo-Saxon" refers to a language as well as a culture. In the Early Medieval period, Latin was the language of the courts and of scholars in all of Europe except England. In England, although monks used Latin, there was also a tradition of writing literature in the vernacular, that is, the language that was spoken—Old

English, the language of *Beowulf.* "Hwæt we gar-dena in geardagum þeodcyninga þrym gefrunon," the poem begins, in words that are impossible for a speaker of modern English to read without study. ("Lo, we have heard of the glory of the Spear-Danes, of the kings of those people in the old days," the lines read, more or less.) Even the alphabet looks strange to us.

The phrase "High Middle Ages" usually refers to the period between 1100 and approximately 1300. But the term is fluid and depends partially on the geographical location being discussed. It includes categories such as "Gothic," a word used by art historians to describe the architectural and artistic styles found in Europe from the twelfth through the fifteenth centuries. Feudalism was the dominant social structure during this time (although it began developing two centuries earlier). This was also when European countries besides England developed traditions of writing in their own vernacular languages, such as Old French and Middle High German. In England, the language was now Early Middle English, which is difficult for modern readers to understand, as these lines demonstrate: "When þe nyhtegale singes þe wodes waxen grene. / Lef ant gras ant blosme springes in Aueryl, I wene" (When the nightingale sings the woods become green. Leaf and grass and blossom sprout in April, I hope).

Like the phrases "Early" and "High Middle Ages," "Late Medieval" is also imprecise. One specific date won't do: In some places, things we associate with the Middle Ages lasted longer than in other places, and the Renaissance began earlier in Italy than in England. But in general, we can say that the fourteenth and fifteenth centuries belong to the category, the Late Middle Ages. We often associate with this era two horrors—the bubonic plague and the Hundred Years' War—but it would seem more fair if we also remembered Boccaccio, Chaucer, and other writers whose names are less familiar but who wrote splendid works in the vernacular during this time period. Or the changes in governmental systems: not only the nobles and the clergy, but also the commoners were represented in France's Estates General in 1302, and across the Channel, Parliament opened in English for the first time in 1362. This English is Chaucer's Middle English, which Modern English readers can understand with only a little trouble: "This world nys but a thurghfare full of wo, / And we been pilgrymes, passynge to and fro," wise old Egeus says in *The Knight's Tale* (lines 2847–8). The end of the Late Medieval Era was also the age of the development of moveable type and book printing.

The words "Middle Ages" imply a time between two eras, the Roman Empire and the rebirth of Roman culture in the Italian Renaissance. However, tell a twelfth-century Parisian scholar like Peter Abelard that Roman learning is dead and you'll get a surprised look—that is, if you can pry him away from his study of Greek and Roman historians and philosophers. Abelard and his contemporaries used the word *modern* to describe themselves. The big lie perpetrated by the Renaissance Italians, who said everything was dark and barbaric until they reinvented Rome, shows how little they knew about the transmission of thought, culture, and learning in the medieval period. While it's true that the vast majority of people didn't participate in all of this learning, neither did the majority of Romans. Nevertheless, classical learning did survive the fall of Rome, and the Latin language remained a living language, the language of learning, well into the Renaissance.

This brings us to back to Velveeta cheese, since in some ways the medieval period *is* remarkably the same no matter how you slice it. One of these ways is the predominance of the Catholic Church, which was largely responsible for the continuance of Latin and learning. In the western part of Europe in the Middle Ages, before the Reformation gave us the Protestant Church, there was only one Christian church, the Catholic Church, which was headed by the Pope. Although there were Jews, they were persecuted and misunderstood, used as scapegoats for all kinds of social ills. Many Muslims lived in Spain, and their learning, like Jewish learning, contributed enormously to medieval scholarship. In the east, the Byzantine Orthodox Church held sway. But for the majority of western medieval Europeans, Roman Catholicism was the only religion, and it also largely defined the social order.

Medieval writers divided society into three groups, those who fight, those who pray, and those who work. The fighters were the nobility, whose responsibility it was to defend everyone else from human enemies. Defense from supernatural enemies, headed by the devil, came from those who pray, the large and varied group of people formally associated with the church: monks, nuns, friars, priests, clerics, and on and on. The workers were everyone else—the men and women who tilled the land, made the plows and swords, brewed the ale and sold it, tended the sheep and spun their wool—and all the other tasks that keep an agricultural society fed and functioning. Within each of the three social groups there were many levels and divisions, from the poor country knight and lady to the king and queen, from a lowly parson to an archbishop, from the serfs, bound to the lord's manor, to the wealthy farmers. The vast majority of the population fit into the last group, those who work, which also means that for the vast majority of people, life was rural and agricultural. It was almost impossible to change your social standing: A peasant was forever a peasant. In rare cases, a boy (but not a girl) might raise his fortune through the church, but the social structure was rigidly hierarchical. Pulling yourself up by your bootstraps wasn't an option.

Another element that unites the entire Middle Ages is the absence of printing. We are so surrounded by books and newspapers, by printed records of every type, that it's hard to imagine a world where every single book had to be painstakingly copied by hand, letter by letter. This meant that literacy wasn't even a fraction as common as it is now, and that it was valued in a very different way. Not until the 1450s did Johann Gutenberg use moveable type to print bibles in Germany, and not until 1476 did William Caxton bring the same technology to England. So from beginning to end, the Middle Ages were a time of manuscripts, or writing done by hand.

The Middle Ages were as rich and wonderful, as cruel and difficult, as colorful and quirky as any other period in human history. The novels discussed in this book illustrate the wonders as well as the hardships of medieval life, and span much of the medieval period, from Anglo-Saxon England to late medieval France. The crash course in medieval culture and history continues in individual chapters, where some historical figures and time periods, as well as specific topics such as literacy, religion and religious diversity, gender roles, and education, are covered in more depth.

The Organization of the Book

In Chapter One I discuss how some writers of adolescent literature forego accuracy in an attempt to provide good role models for readers in their portrayals of books, reading, and the acquisition of knowledge, particularly medical knowledge. The second chapter explores a similar issue: portrayals of religion and religious diversity. Again, some writers' moral sensibility leads them to, in Katherine Paterson's words, "sanitize the past." Other writers work hard to remain true to a past that had a different moral perspective than ours. The same may be said of the writers whose books are explored in Chapter Three: In retelling medieval tales, some present the original tales in appropriate contexts while others allow their didactic tendencies to overtake them. Writers choose a variety of ways to incorporate medieval literature within their own novels, and I discuss several of their techniques. Within these three chapters, readers will be introduced to the roles literacy and religion played in the medieval period, to scribal practices, to medieval antifeminism, and finally, to several medieval literary works.

Chapters Four and Five focus on historical events and characters. First, the end of Anglo-Saxon England and the beginning of the Norman period as they are presented in several novels demonstrates the role of historical ambiguity in the novelist's art. History is always open to interpretation, and when few records exist to be interpreted, novelists are more free to invent. Likewise with historical figures: In both Chapters Four and Five I show how the existence of documentation—or the lack of it—about a particular figure constrains or liberates the writer. The vast amount of evidence concerning Abelard and Heloise,

St. Francis of Assisi, and Joan of Arc, discussed in Chapter Five, contrasts with the scanty documentation available about Harold Godwinson, the last king of England before the Conquest, and William the Conqueror. In these two chapters, readers will learn about a particular medieval period and place, or else about a medieval person, and about topics like gender, education, and the counting of days in the Middle Ages.

Chapter Six turns to the problem of defining historical fiction in order to distinguish it from fantasy fiction. Focusing on two fantasy novels, I compare history with fantasy to help readers draw distinctions between the two. Finally, the Appendix takes the novels introduced within the chapters into the classroom, offering practical suggestions for teachers.

The Novels

Some of these historical novels receive a full discussion, others a shorter treatment. The numbers after each novel indicate the chapter(s) in which it is discussed. On the timeline, a question mark after a novel title indicates that the book does not have a specific setting, but can be placed more generally within that century.

Elizabeth Alder, *The King's Shadow* (3, 4)

Karleen Bradford, *There Will Be Wolves* (1, 2)

Michael Cadnum, *In a Dark Wood* (3)

Karen Cushman, *Catherine, Called Birdy* (1, 2)

————, *The Midwife's Apprentice* (1)

Barbara Dana, *Young Joan* (5)

Nancy Garden, *Dove and Sword: A Novel of Joan of Arc* (1, 5)

Joan Elizabeth Goodman, *The Winter Hare* (5)

Marie D. Goodwin, *Where the Towers Pierce the Sky* (5)

Geraldine McCaughrean, *A Little Lower Than the Angels* (2)

Eloise McGraw, *The Striped Ships* (4)

Scott O'Dell, *The Road to Damietta* (5)

Katherine Paterson, *Parzival: Quest of the Grail Knight* (2, 3, 6)

Gloria Skurzynski, *Spider's Voice* (5)

————, *What Happened in Hamelin* (2)

Mary Stolz, *Pangur Ban* (3)

Rosemary Sutcliff, *The Witch's Brat* (4)

Frances Temple, *The Ramsay Scallop* (2, 3)

Ronald Welch, *Knight Crusader* (2)

DATE	TIMELINE	NOVELS
410	Alaric sacks Rome	
c.450	Germanic invasions of Britain begin	
597	St. Augustine brings Christian mission to England	
c.630	Birth of Islam	
730	Bede writes *Ecclesiastical History of the English People*	
787	Viking attacks on England begin, monastery at Lindisfarne sacked	
800	Charlemagne crowned Holy Roman Emperor	
813–831		*Pangur Ban*
840	Founding of Dublin by Norwegian invaders	
874	King Alfred the Great crowned	
1000	Vikings reach North America	
1066	Battle of Hastings begins Norman Conquest of England	*The King's Shadow* *The Striped Ships*
c.1079	Peter Abelard born	
c.1090	Heloise born	
1096–1099	The First Crusade	*There Will Be Wolves*
c.1117	Affair between Abelard & Heloise	*Spider's Voice*
1100–1135	Reign of Henry I of England	*The Witch's Brat*
1137	Anarchy of King Stephen begins in England	*The Winter Hare*
1170	St. Thomas Becket martyred in Canterbury Cathedral	

DATE	TIMELINE	NOVELS
c.1185		*Knight Crusader*
1209	St. Francis of Assisi begins Franciscan Order	*The Road to Damietta*
1215	King John signs the Magna Carta	*In a Dark Wood*(?)
1284		*What Happened in Hamelin*
1290	Jews expelled from England	*Catherine, Called Birdy*
		The Midwife's Apprentice
1299		*The Ramsay Scallop*
1307–1321	Dante writes *The Divine Comedy*	
c.1340	Chaucer born	
1348–1350	The plague hits England	*A Little Lower Than the Angels*(?)
1400	Chaucer dies	
c.1412	Joan of Arc born	
1415	Battle of Agincourt	*Young Joan* *Where the Towers Pierce the Sky*
1431	Joan of Arc burned at the stake	*Dove and Sword*
1455–1485	Wars of the Roses	
1469	Sir Thomas Malory finishes *Le Morte Darthur*	
1476	William Caxton brings printing to England	
1521	Martin Luther excommunicated from Catholic Church	

ECASTING
THE PAST

Chapter One

Manuscripts and Medicine
Portrayals of Books,
Literacy, and Knowledge

In fourteenth-century France a complete Bible cost the same as half a house, or forty sheep, or a team of hired assassins—no small potatoes (Ladurie 1979, 37; 45). So what is the daughter of an apothecary in eleventh-century Cologne doing with her own book of herbs? And in an age when memory and the spoken word were trusted more than writing, why does a French teenager long to read about medicine when she can learn by working with a surgeon? Writers of adolescent literature have long used medieval settings for their novels. In so doing they have often perpetuated anachronistic fallacies, allowing their didactic tendencies to overshadow historical accuracy. Several recent novels set in the medieval period, while well-researched, unintentionally reinforce misconceptions about books and literacy in the Middle Ages.

These novels span the high and late Middle Ages: Karleen Bradford's *There Will Be Wolves* (1992) is set in late eleventh-century Cologne; Karen Cushman's *Catherine, Called Birdy* (1994) and *The Midwife's Apprentice* (1995) move us to England of the thirteenth century, and Nancy Garden's *Dove and Sword: A Novel of Joan of Arc* (1995) takes place in fifteenth-century France. In some measure, each novel concerns the transmission of medical knowledge. Each has likeable, resourceful characters, wonderful role models for readers, and each book is accurate in most of its details about the Middle Ages. Nevertheless, modern attitudes creep into the stories in the portrayals of reading and learning.

Our bias in favor of literacy is so strong that we often overlook or look down upon other ways of learning, ways that can be equally valid.

When we want to learn about a subject, we go to the library. We look it up. We search it on the Web. But whatever we do, we read about it. For modern audiences, reading is an essential way of gaining knowledge. We value literacy and equate it with civilization. In the Middle Ages, however, especially before printing came to Europe in the fifteenth century, books were only one of many ways of storing and gaining knowledge. Reading was not nearly as common as it is today, and it was valued differently. You didn't need to own a psalter if you wanted to know the text of a psalm; instead, you would rely on your memory or someone else's. Your mother or your nurse taught you your first texts: the Paternoster, the Creed, the Ave Maria, some psalms—but that doesn't mean they knew how to read (Shahar 1990, 210). Even if they did know how to read, they wouldn't necessarily have trusted words their eyes saw over words they heard aloud. Michael Clanchy demonstrates that even highly literate government officials preferred oral to written information; in England, it wasn't until the late thirteenth century that bureaucrats seeking information began to refer to written material (1993, 330). Further, Clanchy notes, "Writing was distrusted and for good reason, as numerous charters of the twelfth century in particular were forgeries" (1993, 332). Whereas we tend to trust written documents over oral information, the situation was quite the reverse in the Middle Ages. We rely on our libraries with their encyclopedias, dictionaries, and other books crammed full of information; for a person in the Middle Ages, the memory was her library, filled with bits of knowledge like a honeycomb filled with pollen from different flowers. Nevertheless, some writing was always valued. George Hardin Brown notes that religious texts like the Bible were considered authoritative even by those who could not read them (1995, 109)—the word Scripture itself means "that which is written."

Even books as physical objects differ today from the way they existed in the Middle Ages. Few books had indices or even page numbers, and the very concept of looking something up is modern. We think of single, bound volumes that encompass only one subject: a bible, a novel, a history of England. Yes, bibles were one of the most common books throughout the medieval period, but in the early Middle Ages, rarely does one find a complete bible. You'd have to kill an entire herd of cattle for the parchment—185 calves gave their lives for the *Book of Kells* alone, and it only contains the four Gospels (Meehan 1994, 86). Although complete bibles were uncommon, they did exist. In the time of Charlemagne, about one hundred complete bibles were manufactured at the abbey of St. Martin at Tours between the years 800–850. These bibles were huge. According to paleographer David Ganz, "You can figure that each double page was the back of one large sheep," and approximately 450 sheep were used for each bible (Stanford 1985, 8). Not until the thirteenth century do small, portable bibles become common, when university students begin to use them as textbooks (Katzenstein 1991, 24).

Instead of complete bibles, monasteries, the main producers of manuscripts in the early Middle Ages, would own gospel books, psalters, collections of prayers, sermons and homilies, and other liturgical books. Important texts—genealogies and legal texts such as wills and manumissions—were recorded in important places; often not in books of their own, but in the margins or blank pages of a gospel book or a psalter, a book you weren't likely to lose. Charms, herblore, and medical knowledge, too, were often stored within the margins of religious books, although some books of medicine and many herbals, or books about the properties of plants, do survive.

An entire library could be encompassed within the pages of an anthology. A thirteenth-century friar's miscellany, for example, the vade mecum of an itinerant friar, might contain sermons, confessional material, saints' lives, exemplars and antifeminist tracts, as well as secular love lyrics, bawdy stories, and learned poems—in English, French, and Latin. Digby 86, a famous manuscript housed in the Bodleian Library at Oxford, was copied around the year 1275. Like other friars' miscellanies, it contains songs, stories, verse sermons, exempla, and religious and secular proverbs, written in both French and English. Wealthy private families might own a few books, including what we might call single-manuscript libraries. The Vernon Manuscript, also in the Bodleian library, seems to have been designed for private reading or for reading aloud to a small group. It is a compilation of religious works in verse and prose. Of the books the Wife of Bath's fifth husband, a scholar, owned, the one he read aloud to his wife was his book of wicked wives, an anthology of stories about women who led men astray.

Reading aloud was much more common than silent reading in the medieval period. Even when you read to yourself, you moved your lips and said the words. As Paul Saenger puts it, "To read in groups was to read aloud; to read alone was to mumble" (1982, 379–80). We have pictures of Chaucer reading aloud to a group at court, and the Middle English poem *Sir Gawain and the Green Knight* is divided into four parts, perhaps for four nights' entertainment. Within the poem's text are references to the audience listening and hearing the poem read aloud. Prose was also often composed for oral performance. Not until the fifteenth century does private, silent reading become common for lay folk (Saenger 1982, 410).

Like reading—silently or aloud? privately or publicly?—literacy is also a complex issue. Sometimes to be literate meant to be able to read Latin as well as the vernacular; sometimes only the vernacular. Literacy could indicate the ability to read only or to both read and write.

Sometimes it simply meant you could sign your name. The term covered varying levels of fluency with written language, just as it does today. Often, we aren't sure what a medieval writer means by words like reading, learning, or literacy. For example, his biographer tells us that when King Alfred the Great was a boy, his mother promised a book of English poetry to whichever of her children could learn it the fastest. The book contained beautiful initials, which drew Alfred to it; "Will you really give this book to the one of us who can understand it the soonest and recite it to you?" he asked his mother. He took the book to his tutor and "learnt it" (Keynes and Lapidge 1983, 75). Of course, Alfred won both contest and book. But we don't know whether the tutor taught the future king to read the poetry or whether the tutor recited it aloud until Alfred knew the poetry by heart. In short, we don't know what Alfred's biographer meant by the word *learn*, just as we don't always know what the word *literacy* meant. Clanchy indicates just how hard it is to define literacy in the Middle Ages; in Norman England, "a knight collecting testimony for the county court . . . needed to speak English and French and to read in English, French and Latin," yet the word *illiterati* was used in contemporary documents to describe those who were neither churchmen nor scholars—and therefore, just such a knight could be considered illiterate (1993, 331).

Even the purpose of literacy has changed from the Middle Ages to the present. We read to learn, to explore new ideas, to gain pleasure, and for a multitude of other reasons. One of the primary purposes of literacy in the medieval period, on the other hand, was prayer (Clanchy 1993, 13). Books of hours, for example, not only contained prayers, but were often also illustrated with pictures the owner could meditate upon.

There Will Be Wolves

Considering these differences between medieval and modern books and their uses, it is with surprise that we find sixteen-year-old Ursula, the daughter of an apothecary, consulting a book to find out how to set a bone in Karleen Bradford's *There Will Be Wolves*. The novel gives a modern spin to eleventh-century Europe by its portrayal of practical knowledge. Instead of consulting her father, an herbalist—who would have therefore been a source of medical wisdom—for instructions on bone-setting, or remembering how she had seen other bones being set, Ursula flips through the pages of a book about herbs in order to educate herself. The bone in question belongs to a dog, and Ursula is able to apply the book-knowledge about humans to her canine friend. We may applaud her resourcefulness but at the same time find fault with the book's lack of realism on this point.

The herb-book (written in an unspecified language), and Ursula's facility with it, are problematic. Even if an eleventh-century trades-man's daughter had been literate, she would not have been as familiar with written language or with books as physical objects as Ursula is. When Ursula uses the book, she "leaf[s] through the pages" to find in-structions on setting and mending "a broken bone in a man's arm" (6). Her ease with the use of written language comes as a surprise; she is the daughter of an apothecary who gently disapproves of her reading because the book contains more wisdom "than an apothecary should know." We are never told how Ursula has learned to read, and it is doubtful whether the daughter of a tradesman in late eleventh-century Cologne would have had any formal schooling. If she reads at all, Ur-sula's skills should be rudimentary, yet she exhibits no hesitation with the written word. Like a modern child, she leafs through the pages of her book until she finds the information she needs.

Even the nature of the manuscript raises questions. "A tattered black book" (5), it appears to be bound and thus a complete codex—a very expensive item, no matter how tattered it is. More realistically, Ursula might own a pamphlet consisting of a quire, or sixteen pages. An old monk, Brother Bernhard, gave Ursula the book, and later other monks demand its return, accusing Ursula of stealing it, which is rea-sonable, considering how expensive books were. Yet the monks are concerned not with the cost, but with the contents, which "could be used for evil by the wrong persons" (62). The evil the monks were con-cerned about is likely to have been a matter of the misinterpretation of texts. In the late tenth century, the Anglo-Saxon monk Ælfric feared that translating the Old Testament from Latin into English would lead to just this sort of trouble—by reading the Old Testament without a priest to interpret it for them, men might think they could do some of the same things the patriarchs did, like taking more than one wife (Crawford 1969, 76).

Ursula's father has taught her "all that [he] know[s] of healing herbs and potions," (5) and thus Ursula's early knowledge is orally-derived. That her father would teach her his craft at all is believable; girls as well as boys learned by helping with the family trade (Shahar 1990, 240). Ursula's father considers the herbal inappropriate for an apothecary because it is "for true healers" (Bradford 1992, 5). For Ursula's father, as for Ursula, deeper forms of knowledge seem to be available only through written, not oral, language. Here, Bradford re-veals her modern bias towards the written word since realistically, both Ursula and her father would favor practical information gained from other people and from experience over knowledge gathered from books. For medieval monks and clerics, deeper knowledge of the Bible would come through written exegesis, but practical knowledge of subjects like carpentry or healing would be gained through practical means, not writing. For Bradford, as for her modern audience, literacy is inarguably positive, associated with education, careful thought, personal freedom, and a broad understanding of the world, concepts not nearly so important to a town-dweller in medieval Europe.

Dove and Sword: A Novel of Joan of Arc

This same bias in favor of literacy is present in Nancy Garden's *Dove and Sword: A Novel of Joan of Arc,* as well, but her portrayal of learning is more complex than Bradford's. *Dove and Sword* features an admirable heroine, Gabrielle, and it is remarkably accurate in its portrayal of the customs and village life of Domrémy. Yet like Bradford, Garden also falls prey to the lure of the book. Gabrielle, Joan of Arc's neighbor, is a peasant who is good at herb-craft, which she has learned from working alongside her mother, a midwife. Together, the two have collected and prepared herbs and Gabrielle has assisted her mother at the bedside of pregnant women. This kind of knowledge-gathering accords with what we know about the Middle Ages. In her study of childhood in the medieval period, Shulamith Shahar remarks that peasant children learned by working with their parents. "In the course of these joint labours, and in the conversations conducted as they worked, the cultural traditions were transmitted from father to son and from mother to daughter" (1990, 244). Thus, Gabrielle's early knowledge is practical and believable. Unlike Ursula in *There Will Be Wolves,* Gabrielle is able to set a bone because she knows "what an uninjured arm looked like, and had felt the bones of [her] own shoulder to discover how they went together" (Garden 1995, 28).

Later, however, Gabrielle reveals her desire to learn to read so that she can "study what books there were about healing"; she wants "to learn to tend the sick beyond what [her] mother knew to do" (26). She envies a young nobleman his ability to read and write when he shows her a book of herblore. Gabrielle's desire to learn more about healing and herbs leads her not to the fields to seek out new plants, but to books, which she cannot read. Like a modern child with a report to write, she goes to the library to look up herbs, although in her case, the library happens to belong to a monastery. As with Bradford's *There Will Be Wolves,* a current idea about knowledge is projected onto a story set in the Middle Ages, but Garden's handling of the matter is more subtle.

In the course of her travels, Gabrielle becomes an apprentice to a surgeon, increasing her medical knowledge more credibly, through practice. Yet later in the novel she goes to a convent where she learns to read from Christine de Pisan, who introduces her to medical treatises, especially those written by women. Garden skillfully weaves information about medieval women's accomplishments into her narrative, but in the end, she, like Bradford, seems to be promoting reading by presenting anachronistic details. Yes, there were educated women in the Middle Ages, like Christine de Pisan herself, and the list Christine gives to Gabrielle includes some of the luminaries, such as Hildegard of Bingen and Dame Trotula. But for Christine to tell Gabrielle that she "will be a midwife, physician, and surgeon, too . . . , if books can make it so" (182) rings false: Gabrielle is already a midwife, physician, and surgeon because of her practical knowledge and experience, her apprenticeship under both her mother and the surgeon. Books are important to Christine, who made her living by writing, but in the Middle Ages, books were not the primary means of gaining knowledge, especially medical knowledge.

The Midwife's Apprentice

In Karen Cushman's *The Midwife's Apprentice,* Alyce learns her craft from an accomplished midwife, not from manuscripts. She watches and remembers what the midwife has done, and she recognizes the medicines she grabs off the shelf from "their smell, since the midwife could not write to make labels, and [Alyce] would not have been able to read them even if she could" (15). Yet even Alyce, who has been homeless and hungry, values books and reading more than a girl in her situation probably would have. Once at a fair she is mistaken for someone else, someone who can read, and she feels enormously complimented (31). And at an inn, when she sees a man sitting in a corner writing, she thinks, "He is writing! That is a man who can write!" (76). Over a long winter, the man teaches Alyce her letters and a few words. Although these scenes illustrate Cushman's unintended promotion of literacy, the sections of the novel about Alyce's medical education are more accurate; Alyce relies on the knowledge of an illiterate, skilled woman, not on letters, and the people of Alyce's village value her for her skill in midwifery, not in literacy.

Catherine, Called Birdy

Of the novels explored in this chapter, *Catherine, Called Birdy,* also by Cushman, portrays books, reading, and writing in the most historically accurate way. In this novel the focus shifts from the peasant and trading classes of *There Will Be Wolves, Dove and Sword,* and *The Midwife's Apprentice,* to the manor house, which Birdy's father, a country knight, rules. Medical knowledge resides with the lady of the manor. Birdy learns from her illiterate mother how to make tonics and ointments, and she supplements this knowledge with what she hears from others in her village as well as with her own experimentation. Although the household owns a book in which generations of women have written "recipes and hints and warnings for the doctoring," the book is only mentioned briefly and Birdy rarely uses it. When she does, she substitutes ingredients she prefers for those she finds disagreeable—fish bones and nail trimmings take the place of "larks' wings or boiled raven" (141). In the midst of writing a diary and reading in the little book of saints, Birdy conceives an idea to make her own herbal in which she will write and illustrate her remedies. This sounds more like a project for a modern character than a thirteenth-century one, but Cushman does not make Birdy's plan central to her novel, nor does Birdy equate the project with any scheme to increase her pharmaceutical knowledge. When she records her treatment of her father's alehead and other ills in her diary, Birdy views doctoring as yet another of the tiresome tasks a lady must do, like spinning and hemming sheets.

In one of the most accurate and telling details in the novel, Birdy writes her diary on her father's scraps of parchment "left over from the household accounts" (2). The ink, too, is leftover. Cushman distinguishes between the Middle Ages and the modern period succinctly by not allowing her heroine easy access to writing materials. Birdy once steals a sheet of parchment from her father's supply on which to draw a picture (134), and later, at a fair, buys four sheets of parchment for four pennies, intending to use them for her herbal (147).

Although access to writing materials is difficult, some books are present in Birdy's life, mainly supplied by her brother Edward, a monk. The household listens to the holy books Edward has sent them—St. Jerome, for example, and the story of Christ's Passion—being read during Lent, and the fact that these tracts are read aloud for everyone in the manorhall rings true, since private, silent reading is as much a modern concept as is the availability of cheap writing material. Birdy keeps another book in her room: the little book of saints that she appropriates from her illiterate mother. An illustrated book of saints' lives is a suitable piece of property for a member of the gentry. Collections of saints' lives, like books of hours, were common in Birdy's thirteenth-century England. Like King Alfred, Birdy is first drawn to the book because of its pictures. Perhaps her use of the book does not accord completely with what the monks who made it would have intended: Instead of meditating on the stories and pictures in a prayerful way, she is fascinated by the sometimes gruesome tales of martyrs, for example, and compares her own life to theirs. But neither does Birdy dangle the book from a chain attached to her belt to indicate her wealth or status, as owners of books of hours sometimes did, instead of keeping their focus on the prayers contained within the book's covers.

Language is an issue for Birdy, as it should be in the Middle Ages. Her brother, the monk, "thinks even girls should not be ignorant, so he taught [her] to read holy books and to write" (5). The language he has taught her is Latin. We don't know what language she writes her diary in, and as with any epistolary or diary novel, readers have to accept that Birdy would write so much, and so coherently. But, in comparison to *There Will Be Wolves*, where issues of language are glossed over, it is a relief that in *Catherine, Called Birdy* literacy is presented as a complex issue. When the steward, who writes the accounts in Latin, reads Saint Jerome aloud to the assembled household, he "stumbl[es] over the Latin" (91). Cushman indicates differing levels of literacy within the manor house, from Birdy's illiterate mother to her brother who knows Latin well, to the steward with his reluctant Latin, to Birdy herself, who, when she teaches Latin to Perkin the goat boy, makes up funny Latin sentences—"my father is a beast"—since she has no grammar books with which to teach him (70).

Often in adolescent literature set in the Middle Ages, literacy is oversimplified into a dichotomy: characters are either literate or illiterate. Bradford commits this error by ignoring the different languages that would have been used in books made for monks and in those produced for tradespeople in Cologne, as well as by making Ursula fully literate. Garden shows the issue to be more complicated: Gabrielle is astonished to learn of a woman who not only reads, but writes: Christine de Pisan writes things that other people would read—and writes them in French. Cushman takes the matter further by indicating the differing levels of literacy, in Latin and in the vernacular, that might be found within one household.

Despite so much historically accurate information, however, Cushman, like the other writers discussed here, seems to feel compelled to promote literacy—both through Birdy's reading and writing and her attitude towards them, and, less convincingly, through Perkin's desire to be a scholar. Birdy dislikes another boy who not only can't read but has no desire to, and she values those who value learning, such as Perkin, who she says is the wisest person she knows. Perkin memorizes Latin and French words when he hears them, and Birdy teaches him some of the Latin she knows. He wants to run away from the village to be a scholar, and Birdy supports him in his wishes, even providing him with money. In her Author's Note, Cushman admits that Perkin is unusual in his desire to move "out of [his] place" in the village (165); what she does not admit is that, like Garden and Bradford, she is providing modern audiences with role models who value books.

Ultimately, the portrayal of reading and books in adolescent literature about the Middle Ages may have a didactic purpose, whether or not writers are conscious of such a goal. In an age when, especially in North America, national campaigns featuring celebrities and politicians emphasize the importance of reading, and when literacy is seen as a key to economic independence, status increase, and personal growth, powerful impulses direct our attitudes towards books. According to Michael Clanchy, not until the nineteenth century was mass literacy "promoted by governments . . . in order to ensure that populations could cope with the growing written demands of daily life—in railway trains, factories, conscript armies, and so on" (1993, 332). Yet we tend to think of mass literacy as a moral imperative, and those who can read should read to others and teach them to read for themselves. The writers discussed here look back at the Middle Ages as a time when children have little opportunity to read and when books were hard to come by. These writers present us with characters who must fight for the books, the reading, and the knowledge they desire, characters who see literacy as an avenue towards knowledge and power. These characters become role models for today's adolescents; just as Ursula and Gabrielle, Perkin and Birdy value books as a means to gain knowledge, so ought their audiences. By this unintentional didacticism, the writers commit anachronisms instead of giving us the real Middle Ages. Thus, not only do they underestimate the cultural differences between medieval and modern society, they also underestimate their readers' ability to comprehend and learn from such differences, condescending therefore to both the past and the present.

Chapter Two

Fidelity to the Infidel
Religion and Religious Diversity

Writers of adolescent literature set in the Middle Ages have a difficult task when they want to portray their characters both sympathetically and with historical accuracy, especially when it comes to issues of religious diversity. While some writers are able to successfully bridge the gap, creating characters who are both likable and accurate, others commit acts of unintentional didacticism in an attempt to teach young readers to appreciate those from different backgrounds. These writers sometimes show medieval Christians appreciating non-Christians in an anachronistic way. When characters are reduced to ventriloquists' dummies, speaking the writer's words, readers may find them less convincing, less sympathetic, and far less fun than the characters who speak for themselves. In creating characters, writers need to trust their readers to be thoughtful enough to recognize the cultural differences between the Middle Ages and modern society.

In this chapter I compare the careful portrayal of religion and religious diversity in Karen Cushman's *Catherine, Called Birdy* (1994) with the more straightforwardly didactic portrayal in Frances Temple's *The Ramsay Scallop* (1994). This comparison establishes the background for a discussion of religious diversity in three other novels: Gloria Skurzynski's *What Happened in Hamelin* (1993), Karleen Bradford's *There Will Be Wolves* (1992), and *Knight Crusader* (1954) by Ronald Welch. A different type of book, Katherine Paterson's retelling of a medieval poem in *Parzival: The Quest of the Grail Knight* (1998), shows not only a modern writer's handling of religious diversity; we also see ways the medieval poet presented Christian encounters with non-Christians. Finally, Geraldine McCaughrean's *A Little Lower Than the Angels* (1987) gives us

11

a view not of religious diversity, but of life in the English countryside at a time when Christianity had no competitors for the salvation of souls.

Presentation and Proselytizing: Portrayals of Religious Diversity

Two novels set at the end of the thirteenth century and featuring four-teen-year-old English girls, mark the extremes. Karen Cushman's *Catherine, Called Birdy* shows Birdy as historically accurate and as sympathetic in her dealings with the Jews. Birdy's level of sophistication—or lack thereof—is convincing; she half-believes the stories she has heard about Jews having tails, and she is sorely disappointed not to get a glimpse of them. On the other side stands Elenor, in Frances Temple's *The Ramsay Scallop,* who displays an unrealistic level of sophistication as she discusses religion, first with a heretic and later, with a Muslim. Temple grips the chalk tightly as she teaches her readers that they should accept and try to understand people from diverse religious backgrounds.

Catherine, Called Birdy

In *Catherine, Called Birdy,* Cushman trusts her readers to be more so-phisticated than Birdy, to understand the monolithic faith of medieval Christianity, especially in a country as insular as Great Britain, where there was little contact with non-Christians. She allows her readers to like Birdy in spite of—or even because of—her ignorance of other cul-tures. Birdy becomes our friend as we read, and we recognize in her our own honest ignorance, which may be transformed to wisdom as we grow older. Birdy never thinks to question the social structure of her own community, from which non-Christians are excluded, yet readers are aware of the problems.

Birdy has an open heart and a mischievous temperament. She is excited to see the Jews who find shelter in her father's hall on their way out of England—the year is 1290 and the king has just expelled the Jews from the country. Birdy plans "to hide in the shadows of the hall in order to see their horns and tails" (11). She believes the stories she has heard about Jews and is disappointed to witness neither horns nor tails, "just wet clothes and ragged children" (11). She writes in her jour-nal that the king "says the Jews are Hell-born, wicked, and dangerous," but adds, "He must know some others than the scared and scrawny ones who are here this night" (11). Although Birdy—with some disap-pointment—recognizes the Jews as humans, "[m]uch like Christians" (11), she never questions their beliefs or compares them with her own.

For medieval Christians who were not scholars and exegetes, religion was not debatable, but simply a part of life. When the hours of the day are measured not by the hands of a clock but by the ringing of church bells to signal divine services, when the time of the year is measured by liturgical ceremonies, when your first song is likely to be the Ave Maria, when the priest is a respected and constantly present part of any village, in short, when Christianity is the very cloth of your life, not merely threads woven into it, you are not likely to stand apart from your beliefs to examine them critically. Imagine a frog trying to describe dry land to a fish, as one does in a story from the Buddhist tradition that explains the difficulty of trying to describe nirvana to those who have never experienced it: "It's not like water" isn't very helpful. As a fish breathes water, not air, so Birdy breathes Christianity. Life without it is unimaginable.

Cushman acknowledges the lack of religious diversity and tolerance during the Middle Ages in her author's note:

> Blasphemy was not only a sin, but also a crime. Almost everyone loved God and worshipped Him in the same ways at the same times in the same kinds of places. The Church said God hated those who didn't—heathens, heretics, pagans, and Jews—so they were slaughtered in His name. (167)

Birdy does not think in any depth about the reasons the Jews are leaving England. Particularly, she doesn't question their persecution by Christians. Instead, she thinks of herself and her desire for adventure. Curiosity about something different motivates her. Because of this, readers can cringe at her behavior, but also identify with her: Who among us has not acted stupidly, often with the best of intentions? Who among us has not unthinkingly demonstrated some sort of prejudice? When we cringe for Birdy's behavior, perhaps we remember and cringe at our own shortsightedness, which we only recognize much later. Birdy tells the old Jewish woman who shelters in her father's hall that she "would rather go crusading like [her] Uncle George" than live her boring life of "sewing and brewing and doctoring" (13). It doesn't occur to her that one purpose of the Crusades was to slaughter the infidel, nor does she sympathize with these particular Jews for being mistreated. Instead, she envies them their journey for the adventure they will meet. Her encounter with the Jews neither strengthens her own faith nor causes her to question it. It does make her question some of the tales she has heard about Jews: "I think some stories are true and some stories are just stories," she says after her disappointment in finding out how ordinary the Jews look and act (12). But when she leaves them, she heads for a harvest fair and looks at a two-headed goat with the same excited enthusiasm she accords the Jews. What she, thankfully,

does *not* do is pedantically summarize all she has learned from her encounter with non-Christians.

In this episode, Cushman does not give in to the modern tendency
to teach readers to tolerate—and respect—diversity. Nor does she
comment on Birdy's behavior. Her use of understatement is admirable:
Cushman respects her readers enough to allow them to see ugly attitudes and to question them. She lets her audience judge Birdy not as a
girl of our time, but as a girl of the Middle Ages who has the values of
her time period. Like Huckleberry Finn, Birdy lives out the form of
Christianity that she has been fed from infancy, a form that sees non-
Christians as agents of the devil—or the devil himself. Like Huck believing that Jim is human without critically assessing the institution of
slavery, Birdy's humanity makes her see the particular Jews she meets
as people without making her accept Judaism. Modern readers can
smile at Birdy's ignorance and compare her actions to our own. We can
also know just what kind of attitudes Birdy would have had she been
born seven hundred years later.

While we can applaud Cushman for her non-didactic portrayal of
religious diversity, Birdy's reaction to the Jews is less intense than most
late thirteenth-century rural English attitudes towards Judaism. As
Robert Worth Frank tells us, "it is an unhappy fact that anti-Semitism
was endemic in the late Middle Ages. And the Virgin was the arch-
enemy of heretics, and of Jews" (1986, 154). In the twelfth century, the
monk William of Malmesbury attacked Jews as "infidel" and "accursed"
in his *Miracles of the Virgin*. His collection of miracle stories, a common
medieval genre, "reflect[s] the popular reaction to the explicit denial by
Jewish writers of the whole doctrine of the Incarnation, which many
Christians saw as a cruel and obscene personal challenge to the Mother
of God" (Chibnall 1984, 160). Chaucer's *Prioress's Tale* is another Miracle
of the Virgin: Remember the little Christian boy who wanders through
the Jewish quarter singing a hymn to the Virgin, "*O Alma redemptoris
mater*"? The Jews cut his throat, but because of his innocent piety, Mary
allows him to keep singing until he can be found at the bottom of the
privy, where the "cursed Jues" have cast his body (PrT line 599). *The
Prioress's Tale* was often connected with the story of St. Hugh of Lincoln,
a child who was supposed to have been murdered by Jews in 1255 and
whose "story is preserved in the ballad 'Sir Hugh or the Jew's Daughter'," as well as in collections of saints' lives (Benson 1987, 916). So in
both courtly and popular literature of the twelfth through the fifteenth
centuries, in both the oral and written traditions, the Jews were reviled.
These are the kinds of stories Birdy would have heard, and heard un-
questioningly, like a white child in the Jim Crow South hearing jokes
and stories that reduced blacks to sub-human status. Taken in this light,
Birdy's reaction to the Jews she meets is mild indeed.

The Ramsay Scallop

In *The Ramsay Scallop*, Elenor reacts not to Jews but to a heretic and to a Muslim. Like Birdy, Elenor too has an open heart. She is admirable and likable, and she wants to know more than her village in England contains. She drinks in knowledge thirstily as she travels the Pilgrim's Way from England to Santiago de Compostella in Spain. But unlike Birdy, Elenor is too wise to be a convincing fourteen-year-old English girl of the Middle Ages. She welcomes comparative discussions of Christianity, the Albigensian heresy, and Islam, weighing the relative merits of each. She speaks about religion with the shepherd Hassad, a Muslim (or Saracen, as Muslims were referred to by Western Europeans during the Crusades), and questions him about his view of God, hesitating and "not knowing how to ask her question inoffensively" (226). What a modern idea! In portraying Elenor as culturally sensitive, Temple shows her own lack of cultural sensitivity: Thirteenth-century England is as different a culture from modern America as Elenor's Christianity is from Hassad's Islam. Temple presents her thirteenth-century character like an American teenager, and in doing so, she does not acknowledge Elenor's culture, which is vastly different from the modern reader's.

Although Temple acknowledges the medieval English perception of non-Christians when she writes, "In [Elenor's] mind every Saracen had a cutlass at his belt, ready for use at the least insult, and Allah was a foreign term" (226), Elenor's actions belie this perception. We might imagine Birdy dropping into a fighting stance, prepared to defend herself against a devil-spawned Saracen, or at the very least, hiding behind a wall and watching wide-eyed for that cutlass. Elenor, however, smiles and laughs with the Saracen and quickly engages him in conversation about religion, specifically about the nature of God.

Elenor stands apart from her own religion, examining it critically, when she is embarrassed not to be able to explain the mystery of the Trinity to Hassad. Her embarrassment indicates her discomfort in the face of a challenge to her own religion, as if she suddenly realizes that the paradoxes of Christianity are not built upon the rock of reason. In her study of medieval perceptions of miracles, Benedicta Ward remarks that "[e]vents called *miracula* permeated life at every level, but they were so closely woven into the texture of Christian experience that there was no incentive to examine or explain the presuppositions that lay behind them" (1987, 1–2). The same might be said of mysteries such as the Trinity and transubstantiation: Ordinary Christians were not called upon to understand or explain complex ideas better left to scholars and priests, and Elenor's embarrassment bespeaks an unconvincing sense of a person recognizing her own culture from the perspective of an outsider. "The Trinity is a mystery," she admits to Hassad (227), but instead of an admission fraught with embarrassment, those five words alone could stand as a pronouncement of her faith.

Even more unconvincing is her reaction to Hassad's denial of the Trinity. Elenor is not shocked or even taken aback when Hassad tells her that God does not have a Trinitarian nature; instead, she wants to know more about Arabic and about Islam:

> "How do you say, 'There is no God but God?'" she asks.
> "*La ilaha il-Allah.* Try it." . . . It will not make you a bad Christian," Hassad says. (227)

Having your village priest tell you that saying Saracen words will not make you a bad Christian is one thing; having a Saracen, a pagan, one who has just said that God is not Three, tell you this is a different matter. But Elenor does not hesitate to look at things from the Muslim perspective, nor does she doubt Hassad's good intentions. In short, she trusts the fidelity of an infidel over a lifetime of Christian teaching.

When Pierre, another shepherd and a believer in the Albigensian heresy, asks Elenor what she thinks of Saracens, she answers, speaking of herself in the third person, "Nora thinks she has much to learn about the world" (229). Later, she asks Pierre why it is that Christians don't consider Muhammad a prophet (230); her question is an implicit criticism of Christianity. In a world that was seen as "a battleground between God and the devil" (Chibnall 1984, 146), we might more realistically expect Elenor to doubt Hassad's words, especially those blasphemous words about the Trinity, as inspired by the devil. In speaking to Hassad—and to Pierre—she is putting her soul in mortal danger. Keep in mind that Elenor is on a pilgrimage to the shrine of Saint James, the patron saint "of the forces fighting the infidel." According to one miracle story, God himself made James a soldier "to fight for the Christians against the Saracens" (Ward 1987, 113). Yet Elenor, in a way more befitting a modern than a medieval teenager, treats these new ideas not with suspicion but with respect, and uses them to deepen her knowledge of the world.

Hassad shares a shepherd's hut with Pierre Maury, a historical figure. Temple's source for Pierre is Emmanuel LaRoy Ladurie's *Montaillou, The Promised Land of Error* (1979), a portrait of an early fourteenth-century village in Southern France where the Albigensian heresy was strong. Since the beginning of Christianity, various groups—labeled *heretics* by the medieval Catholic church—have splintered off from the main church over doctrinal questions such as the divinity of Jesus or the power of the pope. Throughout the Middle Ages, there were many

different types of heresies, one of which ultimately resulted in the Protestant Reformation. Another heresy was called Albigensianism, a sub-
group of the Cathar heresy. The Albigensians "rejected the flesh and
material creation as evil, affirming two eternal principles of good and
evil." They also rejected "the sacraments, the doctrines of hell, purga-
tory, and the resurrection of the body" (Cross and Livingstone 1974, 31).

Using Inquisition records, in which Pierre Maury and his neighbors
reveal much about their lives, Ladurie has reconstructed a portrait of
the people in and around Pierre's village in the Pyrenees. He details
Pierre's life, and we see how gradual his conversion from Catholicism to
Catharism was, how seductive the missionaries, who promised Pierre
that holy men "would pray for him" (1979, 78), and how interwoven
religion was with matters familial, marital, and economic (79–80). The
heretics describe themselves not as heretics, of course, but "goodmen,"
"Good Christians," and those "of the faith" (79); they refer to other be-
lievers as those having "the understanding of the good" (80), and they
say of themselves that "[t]hey are the only ones to walk in the ways of
justice and truth which the Apostles followed" (81). Even after he has
accepted his new faith, Pierre Maury still occasionally attends Catholic
mass, the rituals of which he had grown up with (85), evidence, if
we need it, of how much messier than a set of rules a person's religion
usually is.

In Temple's version of Pierre's life, religion is simple, and Pierre is
as happy to discuss his religion as Elenor is hers. He tells her that those
of his faith are being imprisoned and burned at the stake—which, for
the real Pierre, was cause for caution and secrecy. Pierre's willingness to
jeopardize his life for the sake of a conversation with a Catholic girl he
does not know is as unconvincing as Elenor's open acceptance of a
heretic. Pierre offers to have sex with Elenor, telling her that in his religion, "love is good if both people like it" (214). *Quelle horreur!* Sex with
a heretic? But Elenor is not horrified, just pleasantly surprised, and realizes "that some part of her would like to say yes" (213). Here, as elsewhere, Pierre is reduced to a caricature of Catharism. According to
Shulamith Shahar, "sexual promiscuity was a regular part of the stereotype of a heretic," yet "there is no more evidence for lascivious behavior among the Cathars than among the Catholics" (1983, 264). In a
short space, Temple trots out everything she has read about Albigensian habits and beliefs and applies them to Pierre, who becomes a type,
a representative of Albigensians, not a fully-rounded character.

Denied sex, Pierre turns easily back to religion, and he and Elenor
discuss their comparative beliefs about the souls of animals and humans:
"The migration of one soul from body to body did not ring true to
[Elenor], but she tried to understand what it was that Pierre believed"

(Temple 1994, 220). Elenor's reaction would be admirable in a modern child, but a medieval teenager would more likely have been terrified to meet someone who could bring her own eternal soul into such danger.

Thomas, Elenor's betrothed, is more convincing in his complex understanding of religious diversity, but only slightly. He has been a crusader and has come to question killing for the sake of religion. Early in the book we learn that as a child, Thomas fought against an imaginary Saracen as he practiced tilting, shouting: "Take that, Muhammad!" and "Die, Saracen" (27). He saw heathens not as people, but as fantastic enemies. In this way, Thomas is realistic. Marjorie Chibnall reminds us that people in Western Europe lived in "almost total ignorance" about the religion of the Saracens; "many even believed that they worshipped Mohammed as a god." The stories about Saracens, Chibnall says, "had far more in common with the Arabian Nights" than with the truth, and "Saracens were not so much real people as a projection into the material world of the demons against whom they waged their spiritual battles" (1984, 151). Not until he journeys to the Holy Land and fights real Saracens does Thomas come to a more complex understanding of religious diversity and of holy wars: He sees other Crusaders becoming mercenaries, pillaging and stealing "in the name of God," fighting against the Albigensian heretics, "killing at the command of the Church entire families who held a different view of Christianity from that of the bishops" (Temple 1994, 29). Thomas returns to England a changed man, ashamed of his actions, his mind full of questions.

Nevertheless, Thomas's sophistication in his discussions with Hassad, the Muslim, is hard to accept. Scarcely have the two met each other than they are deep in a discussion of religion. Thomas has "heard it said before that most Muslims understood their religion better than most Christians understood theirs," and he tries to explain Christianity to Hassad by reducing it to two commandments: "To love God with all your heart and soul and mind, and to love other people as yourself" (Temple 1994, 234). Not only Thomas's willingness to enter into this discussion, but even his explanation of Christianity is problematic. This explanation might work for modern readers, but for Thomas to espouse it rings false. In the mid-fourteenth century, religious instruction for boys was by means of rote memorization of commandments and lists. Chaucer's primer would probably have contained "the Exorcism; Lord's prayer; Hail Mary; Creed; Ten Commandments; Seven Deadly Sins; Seven Principal Virtues; Seven Works of Bodily Mercy," and on and on (Brewer 1978, 40–41), lists to memorize, not to discuss in terms of how they applied to one's daily life, as they might be used in a modern Sunday School class. The focus is on the Christian order of things with God at the top and sinful humanity far below. It seems more likely that

Thomas, a man on a pilgrimage, would focus on the necessity of penance and salvation than on neighborly love in his précis of Christianity.

In order to demonstrate that Thomas is an appropriate husband for Elenor, because like her, he has "a lively, curious, and patient mind" (250), Temple has the two discuss "what each had learned from Hassad" (250). They not only speak of the Koran, with which Thomas is familiar from his travels, but they even practice writing "Arabic letters in the dust when no other pilgrims were around" (249). It is far more believable that the scholar Etienne, rather than Thomas or Elenor, would know of the Koran and its alphabet: The English pilgrims meet Etienne as he journeys to Toledo "to learn about Islam and the world of the Arabs" (249). David Knowles tells us that "from 1100 onwards there was a steady stream of northern scholars into Spain seeking for manuscripts to be translated" (1962, 188), and not only Greek works that had been translated into Arabic caught these scholars' fancy—the Koran, too, had been translated into Latin under Peter the Venerable's direction in the twelfth century. However, although theologians were interested in Judaism and Islam, they primarily used discussions about these religions as a way to strengthen their understanding of Christianity (Chibnall 1984, 156).

Temple's heart is in the right place in her portrayal of religious diversity. Nevertheless, she does her audience a disservice by oversimplifying the attitudes of the medieval period and portraying the late thirteenth century as a time when Christians were tolerant of non-Christians. Better to—like Cushman—portray protagonists as a part of their culture, with its strengths as well as its limitations, and allow readers the pleasure of making their own decisions about Elenor and Birdy and the content of their characters. The convictions readers come to on their own may be stronger than the opinions they are fed predigested. Don't readers deserve this measure of trust?

Compensating for Medieval Attitudes: Christianity and Religious Diversity in Other Novels

While Cushman and Temple represent the extremes, other writers also find themselves struggling to portray religious diversity without turning their characters into modern kids. One problem characteristic of recent novels set in the Middle Ages is that non-Christians tend to be portrayed as too good to be true. The wise old Jewish woman and the sweet little Jewish children who offer Birdy their food in Cushman, and the kind shepherds, a Muslim and a heretic, who save Nora in Temple, are mirrored in the scholarly, kind, and respectable Jews in Bradford's *There Will Be Wolves*, an exciting view of life during the First Crusade. In contrast stands Skurzynski's portrayal of a religious outsider in her lovely and thoughtful novel, *What Happened in Hamelin*, in which a non-Christian comes to a thoroughly Christian town. Skurzynski does not fall victim to the kind of oversimplification that may be an attempt to compensate for the medieval rejection of otherness. Instead, she meets the problems of religious diversity honestly and gracefully. Ronald Welch's *Knight Crusader* also gives an authentic picture of the mingling of religions and cultures—: in this case, in the Christian kingdom of Jerusalem. Skurzynski, Bradford, and Welch each portray interactions amongst Christians and non-Christians in their novels, giving readers views of Gypsies, Jews, and Muslims. The interactions in Skurzynski's and Welch's works, however, seem more authentic than those in Bradford's novel.

What Happened in Hamelin

In *What Happened in Hamelin*, Skurzynski weaves historical fact and legend together to tell the tale of the Pied Piper of Hamelin. The setting is thoroughly Christian, thirteenth-century Germany. Geist, a thirteen-year-old, friendless orphan, is befriended by Gast, a stranger to Hamelin, who slowly earns Geist's trust. Like Nora and Hassad in *The Ramsay Scallop*, Geist discusses religion with the stranger, but unlike Nora, Geist has known the stranger for several days and has come to admire him before the conversation takes place. Gast is a man, not a boy, and Geist vies with the other children in the town to be the most important to him. It is only after a strong bond has developed between the two, both outsiders in Hamelin, that Gast speaks to Geist about his religion. The boy reacts slowly, over several days and several chapters, thinking about the stranger's words, "I am not a Christian" (27).

Because it is only one of many parts of the story, and not the focus of a single episode, as it is in Temple's novel, the encounter between Christian and non-Christian has more time to take shape. First, the boy Geist thinks of Gast's safety: "One thing was certain, I would never tell anyone that Gast was not a Christian, or they'd run him out of Hamelin." Geist wonders just what Gast is: "A pagan? An idolater?" He has heard "merchants talk about trading with Jews," but he doesn't think Gast is a Jew (28). During the time Geist is thinking these thoughts, the stranger is taking care to ally himself closely with the boy against the enemy, the baker, who mistreats Geist. In this way, Geist comes to trust and rely on Gast, "even if he wasn't a Christian" (30). In one episode, Geist watches in wonder as nothing happens when Gast willingly enters a church (54–55). This touch seems particularly believable: An uneducated boy like Geist would expect an active God to strike down a non-Christian who entered a holy place.

Twice, the stranger Gast delays a discussion about his religion when Geist questions him (44, 48). When the conversation about Gast's religion finally does come up, fully halfway through the novel, the information is tied up with the boy's pride in being singled out by the stranger. He alone, from among all the children, has been entrusted with a secret, which he will hold "like a treasure inside [him]" (85). Gast tells him both about his background and his religion, which identify him to the modern reader as a Gypsy. "I am no longer Gast, a stranger to you," the man tells the boy. "I am Rom, of the tribe of Rom." "He had given me a part of himself that he had given to no one else," Geist says to himself (86). Because Skurzynski carefully creates an atmosphere of trust between the two characters before this conversation takes place, it has the texture of real cloth, not fairy silk slipping through our fingers.

Some of Geist's questions would be difficult to believe had Gast not worked so hard to gain his confidence. "Do you believe in God?" the boy asks. "Not your God," Gast replies, and Geist responds "so cautiously that [he] almost whispered, 'Then what god?'" (85). Geist's trepidation rings true, but his question, "Do you believe in God?" would not have been believable had it come from any of the other village children, or had Geist asked it earlier in the novel. God is not something medieval Christians chose to accept or reject. In the medieval mind, not *believing* in God is simply not an option. But the discussion of religion is only the surface of a multi-faceted work, and it is designed more to help readers define Gast than to teach us to accept religious diversity. After all, Gast is the Pied Piper, and readers are aware that he is playing Geist the way he plays his silver flute. He will soon lead 130 children out of Hamelin, never to be seen again. In sharp contrast to Temple's and Cushman's portrayals of non-Christians, not being part of the mainstream does not necessarily make you good in Skurzynski's book. For her, actions, not religion, define a character's morality.

There Will Be Wolves

Karleen Bradford's *There Will Be Wolves* is also set in Germany, two centuries earlier than *What Happened in Hamelin*. But instead of a small town like Hamelin, Bradford's book takes place in the city of Cologne, in 1096. Built into the background, the First Crusade, are questions of religious diversity. The purpose of this crusade, known as The People's

Crusade, was to win Jerusalem back from the Turks. Not only Muslims are at issue in this novel, however; within the first chapter a Jewish boy and a Christian girl encounter each other.

Sixteen-year-old Ursula, whom we met in Chapter One healing the broken leg of a dog, lives with her father, an apothecary, in the house attached to his shop. The boy, David ibn Shaprut, is the son of a goldsmith and nephew of a rich merchant. As she introduces David, Bradford also introduces her readers to a little of the history of Jews in medieval Europe, and provides information about the events that will lead to the First Crusade:

> Cologne had been an important center of trade since Roman times, but ever since the Turks had closed off the trade routes to the East, the merchants were having difficulty. The Jews, in particular, were affected by this, as by Germanic law they were not allowed to own land—not even the land their own houses stood upon—and many of them depended on trade. . . . [M]any of the Jewish merchants had had to resort to moneylending to survive. Many of their Christian fellow townsmen despised them for it. Usury was a sin, according to Christian teachings. (11–12)

Bradford goes on to say that many Christians were "deeply in debt" to these Jewish moneylenders (12); in this passage she details some of the roots of medieval anti-Semitism which will play a large part in her novel.

Like Cushman and Temple, Bradford falls victim to the tendency to portray Jews as necessarily good. She draws a false dichotomy between Christians, almost all of whom are characterized as dirty, ignorant, and malicious, and Jews, who are clean, learned, and kind. In doing so, she reveals her bias in favor of the Jews, perhaps in an attempt to compensate for medieval attitudes towards religious diversity and to teach her readers to value non-Christians. Like Temple, she oversimplifies, making her Jewish characters less humans than types for all Jews.

Ursula, who is a Christian, is disliked by her Christian neighbors because she is different from them. Not only can she read, she also washes frequently—but her pride may be what makes the neighbor women hate her most. They finally find an opportunity to accuse Ursula of witchcraft, and the monks and archbishop who try and condemn her are as negatively portrayed as the Christian women. The Christian prophet, Peter, who leads the Crusaders out of Cologne, is also a highly unsavory creature. Ursula and her friend Bruno question his sanity, as does the reader. Of all the characters in the book, only three Christians, Ursula, her father, and Bruno, are positively portrayed, whereas all of the Jewish characters are painted positively. In an attempt to combat negative medieval stereotypes of Jews, Bradford has created her own set of religious stereotypes instead of presenting readers with fully-rounded characters. In addition, she falls unwitting victim to the same malady that infects many writers of historical novels set in the Middle Ages. By painting their protagonists as outsiders who are distrusted by the general populace because of their cleanliness or knowledge or literacy, they imply that the main character is like us, but the general medieval population is unlike us: dirty, ignorant, and mired in superstition.

Knight Crusader

The Crusades form the basis for an older novel, Ronald Welch's *Knight Crusader*, as well. Published in the 1950s and set in Outremer (the Christian kingdom of Jerusalem) in the twelfth century, the novel portrays the complex attitudes towards race and religion of those who have long lived outside of Europe. The main character, Philip d'Aubigny, seventeen years old at the novel's beginning, is of Norman and Welsh noble blood but has lived all of his life in Outremer. He watches with scorn as new recruits from Normandy grow sunburned in the Holy Land and as they insult infidels. For Philip, class and knightly status are sometimes more important than race and religion; he easily slaughters a Saracen robber, who is described this way: "He was a repulsive figure, filthy, pockmarked, his robes stained with dust and dirt, and his head swathed in a grimy turban" (14). Phillip splits the Saracen's skull with his sword, and then watches in satisfaction as one of his compatriots shoots a second Saracen, who "flung up his arms, [and] yelled like a fiend in torment." When the Saracen falls, he becomes "an untidy bundle of dirty white robes" (15). In Philip's view, these Saracens deserve death not because of their religion, but because they are thieves. Sir Jusef, the "Infidel" nobleman they are robbing, is a nobleman and a knight, and so he becomes an honored guest in Philip's father's castle. European knights who have recently come to the Holy Land have come to fight the infidel and do not understand Philip's lenient attitude towards non-Christians.

Philip himself has grown up in a place inhabited by a variety of people. His appreciation for diversity stands in marked contrast to Nora's in *The Ramsay Scallop*, who would have never seen a Saracen before meeting Hassad. Philip, on the other hand, has Syrian servants, and in Jerusalem, encounters all kinds of people. In the marketplace,

> the extraordinary variety of races and types which thronged Jerusalem filled him with delight. He saw Jews shuffling by in long drab clothes of grey, Greek priests with unkempt hair and fluttering skirts of black, and bearded Armenians in tall, pointed hats, chatting in groups at the corners of the narrow alleyways. Eager pilgrims pushed their way through to see the famous buildings and shrines of the city,

while strings of camels padded silently over the cobbles, dark-skinned Negroes from Egypt perched on their backs, guiding the patient brutes with taps from short sticks on their swaying necks. (34)

Like other crusaders, Philip and his father are full of contradictions. Although their very purpose in Outremer is to win it from the Turks, over the years many Crusaders became wealthy and comfortable, holding rich lands that they did not want to lose by fighting. Whereas newly-arrived Europeans might be filled with hatred for non-Christians, the knights who had lived for years, or even their entire lives, in Outremer see a more global perspective, albeit a perspective tinged by self-interest.

In Philip's view, Christians are a varied lot: the Knights Templar and Knights Hospitaller, the monks whose purpose it is to save the Holy Land from the grip of the Infidel, are fanatics. They are, in Philip's opinion, too eager to rush into battle if it means slaying infidels. Other Christians are more careful planners of battle; yet for all of them, war is a way of life. Philip respects many of the Turks he meets and he adopts some of their habits, including bathing regularly and wearing clothing suited to the hot climate. Because he has lived all his life in Outremer and has lived alongside such a diverse group of people, he speaks and writes Arabic fluently.

Unlike more recent novels in which events are told by first-person narrators or else from a limited third-person perspective, the narrator in *Knight Crusader* is undistinguishable from the author. Whereas recent novelists tend to put mini-history lessons into the mouths of characters or find other ways to provide readers with necessary exposition, Welch frequently steps in to comment on the differences in medieval and modern culture, or else on the unique culture of Outremer. Bradford is more like Welch than her contemporaries in the passage quoted above, where the narrator—not a character—provides background information about the Jews. Despite being written in the 1950s, Welch's portrayal of religion and attitudes towards religious diversity is admirable.

A Medieval Portrait of Religion:
Parzival: The Quest of the Grail Knight

Readers interested in medieval writers' portrayals of religion might look at Katherine Paterson's retelling of Wolfram von Eschenbach's thirteenth-century Grail romance, *Parzival* (1961). Paterson takes a hands-off approach to issues of Christianity and comparative religion, as does Wolfram. Paterson is fortunate in her choice of Parzival as a protagonist. Wolfram calls him "a brave man slowly wise" (1961, 5); he is young and simple and has much to learn through the course of the work, just as characters in modern coming-of-age novels do. And, like those modern characters, Parzival reminds us of ourselves and our own indiscretions. Like Elenor, he takes a physical journey that leads to inner change; like Birdy, his ignorance is part of his charm. And also like Birdy, Parzival does not spend much time pondering religion. When young Parzival asks his mother what God is, she tells him that God is "King of Heaven" and that he "made the world and in his love took human form to save it. You must pray to him and ask his help." She goes on to tell him of the devil, the "lord of Hell." Parzival does not think about these words, he simply takes them "to heart," as a good medieval Christian should (1961, 6).

The medieval poem is long and complex, and Paterson scales it down by omitting the sections about Parzival's father and about Sir Gawain. The omission of the first two books, which focus on Parzival's father, Gahmuret, means that Paterson does not have to include passages that might make a modern audience uncomfortable. Wolfram's ambivalence towards infidels in this section of the poem reflects some of the ignorance about non-Christians discussed earlier. Gahmuret, a Christian, ventures into heathen lands, typically—for medieval romance—fantastic in location and name. (Marjorie Chibnall's comment about the medieval equation of Saracens with stories from the Arabian Nights is apropos here.) Gahmuret falls in love with a heathen woman whose "innocence was a pure baptism" (17), marries her, and later leaves her—pregnant with a son, Feirefiz. Wolfram implies no criticism of Gahmuret who, as a Christian, owes nothing to an infidel. Shortly afterwards he marries again, this time to the Christian Herzeloyde, who tells him that "the sacrament of baptism has superior power" over marriage to a "Moorish woman" (53). The poet and the audience must have agreed since Herzeloyde and Gahmuret become the parents of Parzival, the knight chosen to achieve the Holy Grail.

Although she leaves out Gahmuret, Paterson does include Feirefiz in her version of the tale. After growing up and learning wisdom, Parzival meets his heathen half-brother, who is introduced as "an infidel king" (112). Despite the fact that the tale is explicitly Christian, Paterson's characters do not discuss Feirefiz's faith, as they might have done had Temple retold this tale. For Parzival, as a medieval Christian, knowing that Feirefiz is an infidel is enough; he has no need of an explanation of his half-brother's religion. The first two books of the poem, the ones Paterson omits, demonstrate Wolfram's tenuous grasp of what infidels are, just as Wolfram's description of Feirefiz's baptism illustrates that he may have only a surface understanding of the Christian sacrament: "'If I come to baptism for your sakes, will baptism help me in love?' asked the heathen son of Gahmuret" (1961, 424). Promised that baptism will indeed aid him in his quest for love—and the love of a particular woman—he vows, "'Whatever I have to do to have the girl . . . that I will do, and faithfully'" (1961, 425). Feirefiz is baptized and immediately gets the girl: "When the heathen had received baptism and his baptismal garment had been put on him, he waited impatiently for them to bring him the maiden. Then they bestowed Frimutel's child [said maiden] upon him" (1961, 426). Wolfram knows the outer form of baptism, the garments, but the inner significance seems to elude him. Wolfram is a well-read court poet, yet he does not clearly explain his own religion; compare him with Temple's Elenor, a rural English girl who would not have had much formal education, yet who easily converses about Christianity with non-Christians. The juxtaposition points to Temple's disjointed view of medieval life.

In order to condense and streamline the poem, Paterson completely omits Feirefiz's baptism from her version of the tale. She tells us only that Feirefiz "rose to great honor" and that he married the Grail maiden (123); in her version his baptism is not a prerequisite for the marriage, nor does his son, Prester John (also omitted from this telling), convert India to Christianity. Unlike either Temple or, to a lesser extent, Cushman, Paterson does not seize opportunities to educate her readers about life and religion in the Middle Ages. Nor are her omissions designed to avoid offending modern readers with post-colonial consciences. For Paterson, Christianity is—as it is in medieval life—the necessary background of the story, the parchment on which the words are written, and as such, unnecessary to be remarked upon.

In another matter of cultural sensitivity, Paterson writes with great restraint: Feirefiz's physical appearance as the son of mixed races. Wolfram describes him as being "of two colors . . . both black and white," spotted like a magpie (1961, 33), and later, "like a parchment with writing all over it, black and white all mixed up" (1961, 390). Paterson uses Wolfram's description playfully; Parzival describes what he has heard of his brother: "he is neither black as a Moor nor white as an Angevin. He must rather be pied, a mixture of black and white, though I'm not sure how that can be." When Feirefiz reveals himself to his brother, he "was neither wholly white nor black, but something between the two" (116). The phrase, "I'm not sure how that can be" and this last sentence are the closest Paterson comes, throughout her entire novel, to changing the story in order to make it more acceptable to a modern audience. She avoids the spotted figure of Feirefiz that Wolfram gives us, but still includes the magpie image, so important in the poem.

Paterson seems to be more interested in telling a good story than teaching her readers to be tolerant of difference. She never feels the need to explain or apologize for medieval opinions which might be uncomfortable for modern readers. Like Cushman, she trusts her readers to deal with the differences in culture between the Middle Ages and the present. In so doing, she avoids anachronistic fallacies and gives readers a delightful, historically accurate book.

Christianity as the Cloth of Medieval Life:
A Little Lower Than the Angels

Finally, we return to medieval England, this time during an unspecified date within the late medieval period (probably during the fourteenth or fifteenth centuries), for a look not at comparative religion, but a homogeneous society built around one religion. Medieval Christianity is the canvas on which Geraldine McCaughrean paints her novel, *A Little Lower Than the Angels*, a portrait of rural English life where all of the characters are Christian in thought and word, if not in deed. A group of players in a travelling acting troupe perform mystery plays for lower-class villagers. (For a discussion of this novel in the context of medieval drama, see Megan Isaac's *Heirs to Shakespeare: Reinventing the Bard in Young Adult Literature* [2000].) Eleven-year-old Gabriel is the blonde, blue-eyed angel of the troupe who struggles to understand the true nature of the miracles he and his fellow actors perform: A rural rube, Gabriel believes that a blind man's sight is restored during the play's performance. He even believes the venal playmaster who tells him that Gabriel himself caused the healing. Over time, Gabriel begins to understand the ruse pulled on the impoverished inhabitants of village after village, who give their money and goods to the players in hopes of a similar miracle.

Readers might be reminded of Chaucer's Summoner or his Pardoner, both of whom cheat Christians of their worldly goods in return for a promise of salvation. (Likewise, readers might think of contemporary televangelists bilking gullible audiences of their savings.)

McCaughrean demonstrates, through the unlettered Gabriel, how pervasive Christianity was in medieval England. When Gabriel first sees a mystery play, the story of Adam and Eve in the Garden, he feels a sense of familiarity: "Gabriel knew the story: he could not remember why, but he had always known the story. How many times . . . had he seen stained-glass windows showing the selfsame story?" (9). An uneducated village boy, Gabriel is unable to identify the story as one from the Bible or even as something he has heard in a sermon. It's simply a part of his waking knowledge, the way slogans and jingles from commercials are a part of the background noise of our daily lives. Were he to be asked to explain Christianity, the way Thomas is in *The Ramsay*

Scallop, Gabriel would simply stare in wonder. How do you explain the world? The way you live and think? We're back to the frog trying to explain life on land to the fish.

The architecture of each village, even the social order, is defined by the church in *A Little Lower Than the Angels.* It is of church, not civic, authorities that the travelling players ask permission to perform in each town, and it is an abbot or a bishop or a bishop's secretary who grants permission or denies it or throws the players into prison. The performances themselves sometimes take place on the church steps, just after Mass when there will be a ready-made audience. The players' opposition comes from guildsmen, who perform their own mystery plays in the great Corpus Christi cycles (which are still performed in York). These annual performances of the biblical story demonstrate the intertwining of the church in all aspects of medieval life. In all of these ways, McCaughrean paints a convincing portrait of Christianity's role in medieval English life. It is not something most villagers would have been able to think about objectively. It was simply the way life was—and the way it would have been for Elenor in *The Ramsay Scallop* and Birdy in *Catherine, Called Birdy,* as well.

Those writers who understand the vast differences between a thoroughly Christian Middle Ages and our own age, and who take those differences into account in their novels, allow readers to see that as much as we would like to think so, everybody isn't just like us. No matter how much we want a character we like to share our opinions, wishing it doesn't make it so. In a time when multiculturalism is a buzzword, writers who want to portray the medieval period accurately and responsibly must work particularly hard to create likable characters who have the limitations of their time. It certainly can be done, as Skurzynski and Cushman and others have shown. It just takes a little more work on the part of the writers and their readers. The novels that present Christians encountering non-Christians are both more historically accurate and better fiction when they do not reduce characters to stereotypes based on religion. By creating complex characters, writers allow readers to trust in their own instincts, to puzzle out for themselves the morality of the characters they encounter.

Chapter Three

Tales and Their Tellers
Medieval Literature in Modern Dress

What wonderful tales medieval people told each other—stories of loy-alty, of heroism, of tragedy, of love. According to the medieval ideal, lit-erature should both teach and delight. Many stories from the Middle Ages both entertained and posed moral or ethical dilemmas that we can still puzzle over. Modern writers often incorporate medieval material into fiction set in the Middle Ages, carrying on the tradition of teach-ing and delighting. When contemporary novelists do include medieval texts within their works, they have a responsibility to give their medie-val characters reactions befitting their own times, not ours. Although writers use earlier literature in many, many ways, here I'll discuss tales within tales in Frances Temple's *The Ramsay Scallop* (1994) and Eliza-beth Alder's *The King's Shadow* (1995), a medieval poem as the inspira-tion for Mary Stolz's *Pangur Ban* (1988), allusions to medieval works in Michael Cadnum's *In a Dark Wood* (1998), and finally, the retelling of a medieval tale in Katherine Paterson's *Parzival: The Quest of a Grail Knight* (1998).

The authors of *The Ramsay Scallop* and *The King's Shadow* both use the device of the tale within the tale, creating characters who hear or tell medieval stories and poems. Readers of both novels are intro-duced to less well-known medieval works like *The Song of Roland,* and they come across more familiar stories like *Beowulf* and *The Canterbury Tales* as they might have been told in a medieval context—on a pil-grimage or in a lord's hall—not in a textbook smelling of the classroom. *The Song of Roland* figures in both novels, and *Beowulf* and *The Anglo-Saxon Chronicle* are also included in *The King's Shadow*. In *The Ramsay Scallop,* Temple uses two of *The Canterbury Tales*. Despite their reliance on the same technique, Temple and Alder incorporate tales within their tales in different ways, to different effects.

The Ramsay Scallop

The year is 1299, and Nora and Thomas have been sent by their village priest on a pilgrimage to the shrine of St. James in Spain. Along the way, they meet Etienne, a French student, who entertains a large group of pilgrims by telling the tale of Roland, Charlemagne, and the traitor, Ganelon. Etienne's story is a retelling of *The Song of Roland,* an eleventh-century Old French epic based on a historical episode in the life of Charlemagne. Of course, the historicity of the epic is a bit questionable: The hero must be presented as a hero, mustn't he?

In the poem, Count Roland, alone of Charlemagne's retainers, fights against the Arabs. The enemy is too strong, but Roland is proud and waits before asking for help. Finally, he summons his king by blowing his horn, Oliphant. But because of the treachery of Ganelon, Roland's stepfather, Roland dies before Charlemagne can arrive to help. The poem celebrates "a warrior's loyalty to his fellow warriors and of a man to his lord" (Hanawalt 1998, 42). Historically, the battle at Roncesvalles pitted Christian against Christian, but in the poem, the enemy became Saracen.

Temple's Etienne summarizes the epic in several pages, and other characters interrupt him to ask questions or make comments. The poem glorifies war, and Frances Temple doesn't particularly like it. We can tell because both Nora and Etienne—of whom Temple is fond— dislike it. Nora says to Etienne, "You don't like this story, do you" (171), and later, she falls asleep thinking: "What a chump Roland was. . . . Ganelon was a traitor, but it was he who wanted peace" (175).

In the morning's discussion of the tale, two of the female pilgrims find fault with the idea of heroism presented in the story. Temple wants us to question our own perceptions about heroism—and about who can be a hero. She has Nora say: "In stories the men are heroes because of what they do, but if the women are heroes at all, it is because of what they think, or because of what happens to them" (175). This analysis by medieval people of an oft-told tale seems better suited to an audience of a later age. The only pilgrim who likes the story is a little boy, who wants to hear more about the fighting. Temple comes dangerously close to implying that the story—so popular in the Middle Ages— is childish, and therefore, so were those silly medieval people. For Temple to incorporate the poem into her novel only to deride it is in keeping with her tendency to chastise medieval values, but why pick on a poem that is one of the most enduring of medieval monuments?

Even more enduring and endearing are *The Canterbury Tales.* Although Temple takes one of them to task for not echoing modern attitudes, she is more generous with a second tale. The appearance of Chaucer's tales, composed between 1360 and 1400, in *The Ramsay Scallop,* a novel set in 1299, is less problematic than it might seem: few of his plots were original to Chaucer, and a major strand of Chaucer scholarship looks at sources and analogues for his tales. Travelers such as those in *The Ramsay Scallop* could easily have been familiar with these stories. Their reactions, however, would not be the same as ours, yet Temple treats Chaucer's *Clerk's Tale,* the story of Patient Griselda, the same way she treats *The Song of Roland:* her characters react with modern sensibilities. Instead of interpreting the story the way a medieval audience might, her characters are filled with anger and disgust by the plot the way modern students in a Chaucer class often are.

You can see why. In the tale, Walter, a nobleman, chooses the poor (but of course beautiful) peasant Griselda as his bride. He demands obedience from her, and she gives it to him. However, Walter is never satisfied with his wife. Time and again he tests Griselda's obedience, first taking away their daughter and pretending she has been killed, and later doing the same thing with their young son. Griselda never complains. Finally, Walter sends Griselda herself away, telling her he intends to take a different wife. Before she goes, however, he tells her she must prepare the bedchamber for the new bride, which she does with nary a peep. The bride turns out to be Griselda's own daughter, now grown up. In the end, Griselda is happily reunited with her children and with the now-trusting Walter.

How is an audience to take such a story? A medieval audience might look for allegorical readings, seeing Walter as God and Griselda as the obedient Christian who is willing to sacrifice her child the way Abraham prepared to sacrifice Isaac. The story might work on several levels, one of which would be as an exemplum of wifely obedience. This seems to be the way the Ménagier, or Householder of Paris, as Eileen Power (1924) calls him, saw it. A fourteenth-century Parisian merchant who married a young woman, the Ménagier wrote a book of advice for her about how to be a good wife. It's full of fascinating details like how to rid your house of fleas and how to treat servants; it also contains the story of Patient Griselda as a model of how obedient a wife should be. The Ménagier probably didn't expect his wife to be quite as obedient as Griselda, but neither did he intend to act like Walter. (Tania Bayard's condensed translation, *A Medieval Home Companion* [1991], is a good introduction to the book, as is Eileen Power's chapter, "The Ménagier's Wife" in her older but still valuable *Medieval People* [1924].)

The story of Griselda was popular not only with the Ménagier of Paris. It had many other readers as well, as its survival in so many manuscripts attests; versions of the story in English, French, Italian, and Latin survive. Chaucer's Clerk himself tells us that his source is Petrarch, and we know that Petrarch translated Boccaccio's version (in *The Decameron*) from Italian into Latin. As a folktale, other versions of the story existed long before Boccaccio wrote it down (Benson 1987, 880). Such popularity—with both scholarly and folk audiences—suggests that medieval people would not react with such unqualified disgust as Temple's characters display. "This is a revolting story," Eleanor says, and another woman agrees: "[Griselda's] not a hero, she's a footscraper" (178). Temple's female characters have particularly strong reactions to the tale, and Temple seems oblivious to the differences in attitudes towards women in the medieval and modern eras.

Medieval anti-feminism, like medieval anti-Semitism, is an undeniable fact, no matter how unpalatable it is to us. Women did not enjoy the same status that men did. They were seen as weak, easily distracted, and ruled by the senses, which were untrustworthy and easily controlled by the devil. (To get to heaven it was important to focus on spiritual, not bodily matters like the senses.) With all of these faults, women were thus liable to sin—in fact, they were responsible for it. The origins of medieval anti-feminism are, as Alcuin Blamires (1992) points out, fuzzy and debated by scholars, some of whom trace the idea to "ancient Judaic law," some to early Greek culture (think of Pandora, who because of her curiosity brought evil into the world), and some elsewhere (2). Whatever the origins, both church and secular laws throughout most of Europe in the medieval period prevented women from taking public roles. Women were thought to be less intelligent than men, light-minded, greedy, and wily (Shahar 1983, 12). They were associated with material things, while men were associated with the spiritual (Blamires 1992, 3). Of course there were exceptional women: Heloise, Joan of Arc, Christine de Pisan. But they *are* exceptions, and the general lot of medieval women differed enormously from theirs. Some medieval women may have chafed against these constraints, but that is not reflected in the literature that survives from the Middle Ages, although, as the Wife of Bath says in her Prologue (in a text written by a man!):

> By God, if wommen hadde writen stories,
> As clerkes han withinne hire oratories,
> They wolde han writen of men moore wikkednesse
> Than al the mark of Adam may redresse. (WBProl lines 693–6)

The Wife of Bath is as remarkable as Christine de Pisan, and despite her comment, modern writers need to be careful not to ascribe current ideas about women's roles to medieval characters, as Temple does with *The Clerk's Tale*.

Temple's treatment of characters' reactions to *The Wife of Bath's Tale* is much less anachronistic, partly because the story fits much better with contemporary tastes. According to the tale, when a knight rapes a maiden, Queen Guinevere and her ladies decide that as punishment, he has a year to discover what women desire most. If he fails, he loses his life. An ugly old woman gives him the answer in exchange for his promise that he will do whatever she asks. The answer is revealed— women want control over their husbands—and the old woman demands her reward: the knight must marry her. He is horrified, but the queen requires him to keep his promise. On their wedding night, however, all is revealed: the old woman is really a beautiful young woman who has been enchanted. As befits a fairy tale, everyone lives happily ever after, except the maiden who was raped, but she isn't a part of the story. Only a modern audience would wonder what happened to her, and fortunately, Temple's characters do not discuss her fate (although one woman says "The knight got off too easy" [150]). Instead, they seem to agree with Eleanor's assessment: "'That was a good story,' she said" (150).

Temple gives both tales appropriate tellers: a student tells *The Clerk's Tale*, and an old woman narrates *The Wife of Bath's Tale*. The use of these two *Canterbury Tales*, both of which the Chaucer scholar George Lyman Kittredge (1911–12) included in his "marriage group," or the set of tales within the *Canterbury Tales* that focus on marriage, is fitting in *The Ramsay Scallop*, since Nora's upcoming marriage to Thomas is a theme of the novel. Although Temple misrepresents medieval attitudes, she does a fine job of placing these tales and *The Song of Roland* within the context of a pilgrimage, allowing characters to comment on them, and turning them into quick, lively stories instead of dead ones relegated to a Required Reading list.

Temple simplifies stories, including only basic plot elements, in order to have them not overwhelm her novel. Each tale provides implicit commentary on the novel's thematic elements, and Temple allows readers to discover these connections for themselves. She chooses stories that are easily summarized and she leaves in some parts that are not essential to the plot, but important for understanding the medieval mind. For example, she includes the discussion of *gentilesse* from *The Wife of Bath's Tale*, in which we learn that true gentleness (a word that to a medieval audience signifies high birth) comes from God, not from your family tree.

Nevertheless, her treatment of the works is evidence of Temple's moral stance. She wants to fit the Middle Ages into a Procrustean bed of modern taste, lopping off the parts that don't easily fit. Far better to represent medieval literature by allowing characters reactions appropriate to their own era, as Elizabeth Alder does in *The King's Shadow*.

The King's Shadow

Like Temple, Elizabeth Alder incorporates references to *The Song of Roland* and *Beowulf* into her novel, *The King's Shadow*. (Her use of another medieval text, *The Anglo-Saxon Chronicle*, will be treated in depth in Chapter Four.) However, Alder's purpose in including medieval works differs from Temple's, particularly in the case of the Old French epic. Instead of using the plot of *The Song of Roland* to comment on morality or heroism, Alder celebrates the sound and emotion within the poem. Evyn, an eleventh-century Welsh boy who hopes to be a bard, or *storiawr*, sings the song:

> High are the hills and dark the valleys, brown are the
> rocks and dread the defiles . . . When Roland sees the
> peers, and Oliver whom he so loved, lying dead, pity
> takes him and he begins to weep . . . So great is his
> grief he cannot stand. (3–4)

In Evyn's view, "This was a story of courage and honor and death, worth telling well" (12). Over and over, Evyn chants the beginning, "High are the hills and dark the valleys," lines that resonate throughout the novel, even after ruffians cut out Evyn's tongue and destroy his dream of becoming a *storiawr*. Evyn's story is also one of courage and honor and death. He loses not only his family but his freedom and his purpose in life. By living with courage and honor, his finds a new purpose, regains his freedom, and becomes part of a new family, although death will haunt this one, too.

When Evyn hears a bard singing "The Battle of Brunanburh" (49–50; the poem is recorded in *The Anglo-Saxon Chronicle*), his reaction is personal: He, who can never sing again, should have stood in this bard's place. The significance of the story itself, in which a warrior's "young son [is] mangled by wounds," (50) and its relationship to Evyn's own situation, Alder leaves for the reader to discover. Similarly, when Evyn hears *Beowulf* for the first time, "he listened intently as the storyteller wove magic with words" (207). The poetic passages comment directly on the events in the novel, but Alder again allows readers to make the connections themselves instead of having Evyn comment on them. She allows Evyn to be a boy of his time, the eleventh century; not, like Temple's heroine, a modern teenager transported into the Middle Ages. Alder also illustrates the kinds of stories and poetry Evyn would have told as a *storiawr* by including them within the novel. *The Song of Roland* in particular had an international audience. At the Battle of Hastings, which will take place shortly after the end of the novel, "William I's minstrel-herald, Taillefer, encouraged the Norman army . . . by juggling with his sword and singing the song of Roland, but he was killed in the battle" (Lefferts and Rastall 1998, 516).

Unlike Temple, Alder does not give the reader the entire plot of *The Song of Roland* or "The Battle of Brunanburh" or *Beowulf.* Instead, she presents snatches of poetry. In *The King's Shadow,* the effect poetry has on the listener is more important than what happens in the poem, although in both novels the poems comment in some way on the action of the novel. When a bard sings of Beowulf, he begins not with the beginning, but with the end: the old king's fatal fight with the dragon. A man sitting in King Harold's hall calls out, requesting this part of the story, and the bard sings it with the king's permission. We only hear eight lines of poetry, but in them, we know that Beowulf, now king of his people, will die—as surely as we know that King Harold, who sits listening to the epic, will soon meet his own death in battle. By including poetic excerpts Alder gives readers a taste for more. Those who reveled in the novel may be lured into the library to look for the poems which enticed them.

Alder's use of medieval poetry contrasts sharply with Temple's. Readers who have been introduced to *The Song of Roland* in *The King's Shadow* might well be seduced by the words in the same way Evyn is, leading them to seek out the entire poem. Instead of reducing the poem to a plot summary and then reprehending its values as Temple does, Alder twists poetic lines sinuously around the reader's tongue and through the texture of her tale by her repetition of snatches of the poems themselves. She celebrates poetry and invites her readers to join in the dance.

Pangur Ban

An entire poem is not only quoted in Mary Stolz's delightful *Pangur Ban,* it also serves as the basis and inspiration for the novel. The son of a farmer in ninth-century Ireland, Cormac longs for the monastic life because it offers the chance to learn things and make books, not just to plow fields and mend fences. When he finally achieves his goal, becoming a monk and a scribe, Cormac first copies books written by others before composing his own life of Saint Patrick and the poem that gives the novel its title. We'll probably never know the name or circumstances of the real Irish monk who wrote the poem (in Irish) in the margin of a Latin missal (a book with all the texts necessary to perform the Mass), but Stolz imagines his story as Cormac's. The poem begins:

> I and Pangur Ban my cat,
> 'Tis a like task we are at:
> Hunting mice is his delight,
> Hunting words I sit all night. (136)

Because the brief poem reveals little about the actual life of the writer, Stolz is free to invent a fourteen-year-old boy who shirks his farm-duties to draw and paint mice—while, nearby, his cat stalks them. His unimaginative father finally takes him to the monastery in disgust: if he won't do his work on the farm, maybe he'll do his work as a monk. Cormac embraces monastic life, although to the end of his days, he shirks his duties for his illuminations. His cat, Pangur Ban, accompanies him from farm to monastery when Cormac argues to the abbot that a cat is not a personal belonging (which monks may not own), since "nobody owns a cat. People only think that they do" (95).

Although the real poet wrote in the margin of a manuscript he was copying, Cormac uses a separate sheet of parchment at the end of his life of St. Patrick. We get a sense of what his work might have looked like from the novel's cover and from the illuminated letters that begin each chapter. Although they are more modern than medieval, Pamela Johnson's charming initials incorporate common Irish motifs like geometric shapes and interlace patterns similar to the ones in *The Book of Kells*.

Cormac illuminates his poem, "Pangur Ban," with as much care as he gives the saint's life. He begins with the large majuscule "I" twined about with vines and "adorned with elaborate embellishments and gilt interlacings upon which insects and birds seemed actually to flutter" (136). The poem exalts an individual, not God, which monks were not supposed to do. But they did: The twelfth-century English scribe Eadwine included a full-page self-portrait in the psalter he copied and extolled his own genius in an inscription which begins, "I am the chief of scribes, and neither my praises nor my fame shall die; shout out, oh my letter who I may be" (Heslop 1992, 180).

In the later Middle Ages, when professional scribes, not just monks and nuns, produced manuscripts, the paying patron might be exalted in a way similar to Eadwine. For example, the dedication page of the Luttrell Psalter, a book of psalms discussed later in this chapter, contains a portrait of the patron wearing armor and sitting astride his horse. Heraldic devices identify him as Sir Geoffrey Luttrell, as does the text above the portrait: "Dominus Galfridus Louterell me fieri fecit," or "Lord Geoffrey Luttrell had me made." Sir Geoffrey is showing off just as much as Eadwine is, although he wants people to admire not his artistic and scribal skill, but his wealth at being able to commission such a deluxe manuscript.

Within *Pangur Ban*, Stolz includes yet another way medieval people expressed themselves within books. Stolz quotes a real monk's words: "Thank God, thank God, and again oh again, thank God, I have reached the end of this missal!" (13). Such scribal colophons—inscriptions that tell about the making of the manuscript—are one of the rewards of studying manuscripts. Like the cats watching the mice eating sacred bread in *The Book of Kells* illuminations and the whimsical drawings in the margins of Gothic manuscripts, colophons reveal a tantalizing glimpse of the person who wrote or illustrated the book. "Deo Gratias," or "Thank God," colophons often begin, before proclaiming the scribe's desire for a glass of wine or complaining of his cramped fingers. Cormac uses another formula favored by many monastic scribes and illuminators when he writes "Cormac me fecit" at the end of his poem (137). The book seems to come alive when it speaks in the first-person voice, saying: "Cormac made me."

In addition to "Pangur Ban," other Irish poems and tales are woven into the novel, but they are ones Cormac doesn't like. His mother chants stories of the great hero Cuchulainn and "The Cattle Raid of Cooley" (74), but Cormac is less interested in battles and battle chieftains than he is stories about St. Columba and St. Patrick, the latter of which he will eventually write himself. Several biographies of Patrick survive, the earliest from the seventh century, so it is plausible that Cormac might have written his own version. Stolz doesn't reveal any of the details from those biographies, fascinating though they are.

Viking raids play a large role in the novel, although we only hear about them obliquely, never witnessing the horror the Vikings inflicted on farmer, monk, child, and chieftain alike. The Vikings were brutal and ruthless in their raids. They were not Christian, so they reserved no respect for churches and monasteries, which made them seem especially horrific to medieval Christians. Because churches and monasteries often housed wealth in the form of golden crosses or reliquaries, they were frequently attacked. Readers do not see the attack on Cormac's monastery, but it is clear that although his poem will survive, Cormac himself will not.

The novel ends with a triad of chapters set three centuries after the life of Cormac. When an English monk visits Ireland in 1169, he finds the ruins of Cormac's monastery and thinks about those monks who lived so long ago—300 years or more. Stolz gives a good sense here of how vast the medieval period is by having a twelfth-century character think thoughts similar to ones we might have upon visiting the ruins of a long-ago life. At the same time, a sense of familiarity pervades her novel, since we can still be drawn across more than a millenium to the same ideas that enchanted a ninth-century monk, one who delighted in the company of his cat. Stolz's inclusion of the entire poem in her novel creates a link between then and now and highlights the enduring power of poetry. Like Alder, she obviously loves the poetry she writes about, and she conveys her pleasure to readers, allowing them to share in her delight.

In a Dark Wood

From the tales and legends of Ireland, let us now shift our gaze to the legendary English outlaws who people Michael Cadnum's *In a Dark Wood*. The Robin Hood novel is becoming a genre in its own right: Teresa Tomlinson's *The Forest Wife* (1993) and *Child of May* (1998), Monica Furlong's *Robin's Country* (1995), and *The Outlaws of Sherwood* (1988) by Robin McKinley are recent representatives that follow Geoffrey Trease's 1934 novel, *Bows Against the Barons*. But Cadnum provides a twist— both in his presentation of Robin Hood and in his use of medieval literature. *In a Dark Wood* tells the story of Robin Hood from the unlikely perspective of Geoffrey, the Sheriff of Nottingham. Cadnum cunningly borrows from medieval texts in a surprising way, using bits of well-known tales like puzzle pieces. After you see one allusion, you start looking for others, the way you look through the Sunday-morning cartoon that challenges kids to "find seven things that don't belong in this picture." Once you see the tennis shoe in the apple tree, you can't stop searching for all seven items. But Cadnum neither identifies his sources nor gives the answers upside-down at the bottom of the page; he doesn't even include an author's note. And many of his allusions are so esoteric that only a medievalist would catch them. Unlike Temple, Alder, and Stolz, who incorporate medieval literature *as* literature into their novels, Cadnum stealthily borrows Chaucer's words to describe his own characters. Other borrowings include an idea from William Caxton and descriptions right out of a medieval manuscript. These allusions may not be easily accessible to students but they enhance the layered texture of Cadnum's work.

Early in the novel, a character "used the London word for egg, *ey,* not the local [Northern] *eyren*" (27). Teachers who have studied the history of the English language might recognize this incidental allusion to William Caxton's "Preface to the Aeneid" in which Caxton—living before the standardization of the English language—wonders which form of a word he should print: "Lo, what should a man in these days now write—eggs or eyren?" (1973, 462). (Cadnum makes a small mistake: The different forms of the word in Caxton are *eggs* and *eyren,* not *ey* and *eyren,* which are simply the singular and plural of the London dialectal form. The -en ending is the strong plural form: we still use it in *children, oxen,* and *brethren.*) Caxton's "Preface" is often anthologized in college textbooks such as *The Oxford Anthology of English Literature*, but high school readers would have more trouble locating it.

Perhaps this allusion was accidental. Perhaps not. Consider: A few pages later, Geoffrey speaks to an abbess, who "laughed through her nose, like a Frenchwoman" (30). If the line makes you think of Chaucer's

Prioress, it should. Within the same page the abbess is described in a paragraph straight out of *The General Prologue* to *The Canterbury Tales:*

> Her gray habit was crisp and new, and a band of coral
> ran around her wrist. Every eleventh bead of her
> rosary was jade, and a golden brooch hung from the
> beads, engraved with the letter A. Round the peak of
> the A ran a crown, and in fine letters . . . were the
> words *Amor Vincit Omnia.* (30–31)

Here, the allusion is more straightforward and recognizable. If not before, many English teachers' noses would be aquiver at the familiar scent of the last phrase, "Love Conquers All." Compare the relevant lines from Chaucer:

> Of smal coral aboute hire arm she bar
> A peire of bedes, gauded al with grene
> And theron heng a brooch of gold ful sheene,
> On which ther was first write a crowned A,
> And after *Amor vincit omnia.* (GP lines 158–62)

The doctor, too, is modeled on Chaucer's Doctour of Phisik, and wears "blood-red, slashed with blue, and the lining was shiny taffeta" (51). The description comes again from the *General Prologue,* but it is hardly a Chaucerian passage that comes tripping off every English teacher's tongue: "In sangwyn and in pers he clad was al, / Lyned with taffata and with sendal" (GP lines 439–40). *Sangwyn* means red, *pers* means blue, and that's what the doctor of Nottingham wears. Like Chaucer's physician, Cadnum's doctor is a man of measure who well knows the four humors and the relationship between astrological events and illness, but unlike Chaucer's character, this doctor does not collude with apothecaries, setting the prices of medicines, nor does he profit from the plague.

Later, we meet a miller with wide black nostrils who carries a stave and plays the bagpipe, more allusions to the *General Prologue* of *The Canterbury Tales* (86), thus tempting the reader to see Chaucer everywhere—*The Friar's Tale,* for example, in the sentence: "A wagon was sunk into mud, and a peasant pushed from behind to help the ox" (117). In *The Friar's Tale,* two men, one dressed in green and carrying bow and arrows, come across a carter whose cart is stuck in mud; in the novel, two men, one dressed in green and carrying bow and arrows, see a peasant whose wagon is stuck in mud. In Chaucer, the man in green is really the devil, and the other is a summoner who will shortly be taken to hell; in Cadnum's novel, the two men are Robin Hood and the Sheriff of Nottingham. Whether or not the allusion was intended, paired with the other Chaucerian references, it enriches Cadnum's text, allowing us to look for similarities amongst the characters of the summoner and the sheriff, and the devil (who, in Chaucer, dresses as a woodsman and who comes from the North) and Robin Hood, who has told the sheriff that he has journeyed "from north of here" (104). Is Robin Hood like the devil in Chaucer's tale, who sports with the summoner? Other allusions enrich the text in a similar way: If the sheriff is having an affair with a woman like the Prioress, what does that reveal about his character? Cadnum's touch is light; readers who see the allusions will be pleased, while those who don't will still enjoy the story. And Cadnum doesn't overdo it: The novel's franklin is just a franklin, not "Epicurus owene son" (GP line 336), nor does Sir Roger, the old Crusader knight, look to be modeled on Chaucer's Knight. Cadnum seems to be having fun and inviting his readers to do the same; games and gaming are an important part of the story, so why not make them a part of the texture of the tale?

The novel's texture is further enhanced by possible allusions to a visual source, the Luttrell Psalter, a fourteenth-century illuminated manuscript that contains scenes of rural English life so accurate that they have been used as the basis of an open-air museum in England. In Cadnum's novel, we read, "A horse dragged a wooden frame weighted with a stone, the comblike teeth of the frame breaking the earth into perfect lines" (7). For an illustration of this scene, see folio 171 recto of the Luttrell Psalter, where, in the bottom margin, two peasants are harrowing (Backhouse 1990, 22). It's one of the most famous illustrations in the Psalter, and whether or not Cadnum was consciously referring to it, the description is apt, particularly when the following sentence uses the word "border," making me think of the manuscript's decorated margin. Likewise, within the same paragraph, Cadnum describes a scarecrow as being "like half a man miraculously endowed with the power to fight or at least kill magpies" (7). A reader already alerted to the Luttrell Psalter scene might be reminded of the fabulous creatures who inhabit the manuscript's borders, such as the half-man, half-bird on the top right of folio 208 recto (Backhouse 1990, 48). Later in the novel, Cadnum writes: "A peasant in a black cap the shape of his skull struck a tree with a stick, and acorns fell to the ground. Pigs ate them . . . " (59)—the scene is on folio 59 verso of the Psalter, in the upper left-hand margin, and the man's cap is indeed black and skull-shaped (Backhouse 1990, 16). What other allusions to the Psalter and other works have I missed? (Readers who can't find Backhouse's book on the Luttrell Psalter might look at Sheila Sancha's *The Luttrell Village: Country Life in the Middle Ages;* the illustrations were inspired by those in the Psalter.)

Cadnum's sly references to medieval works bring pleasure to readers who recognize them and heighten the audience's awareness of the dual texts, but play no vital role in the novel's plot. In this way, his technique is reminiscent of Elizabeth Janet Gray's in her 1942 novel for younger readers, *Adam of the Road*. Gray, too, alludes to *The Canterbury Tales* and, as Miriam Youngerman Miller has shown, a variety of other, less well-known medieval texts including *The Proverbs of Alfred, Havelock the Dane, King Horn,* and *The Second Shepherd's Play* (1995, 81). References such as these will only be recognized by those who have studied the literature of the Middle Ages; for Miller, they "provide authenticity to [Gray's] story" (80). Cadnum's story, too, is authenticated by his allusions to medieval works. Even if students don't recognize them, they help to recreate the medieval world convincingly. And readers who do recognize the allusions are provided with the pleasure of unexpected discovery.

Parzival: The Quest of a Grail Knight

Some writers choose to retell medieval tales, not just allude to them. For example, Rosemary Sutcliff has turned both *Beowulf* (in *Dragon Slayer: The Story of Beowulf* [1961]) and *Tristan and Iseult* (1971) into novels. Katherine Paterson does the same thing in *Parzival: The Quest of a Grail Knight*. Her story retells an early thirteenth-century German poem by Wolfram von Eschenbach. The poem, a medieval romance, is often compared to the bildungsroman since it traces the psychological, religious, and moral development of its hero, Parzival, from his early youth to maturity. In this way, the work seems ready-made for an audience accustomed to the coming-of-age novel. Parzival, whom Wolfram calls "a brave man slowly wise," is comically ignorant in the beginning, brought to grief by his ignorance, and finally, after years of questing, finds compassion and wisdom. Yet Paterson, who has previously recast the Parzival story in *Park's Quest* (1988), a modern quest story implicitly structured around the grail quest, had to find a way to retell the medieval poem, with its complex structure and many digressions, in a way that would appeal to her audience. (See Chapter Two for a discussion of religion in *Parzival*.)

The medieval poem is very long and divided into sixteen books, the first two of which focus on the adventures of Parzival's father. Parzival himself isn't even born until the end of Book II. Paterson wisely begins her novel here, with Parzival's birth. She also deletes the parallel tale of Sir Gawain, which is interlaced with the story of Parzival. In the medieval poem, Gawain is the best of the worldly, Arthurian knights, while

Parzival is the best of the Grail knights, who are outside the earthly realm. In the poem, parallel elements in the stories of Parzival and Gawain are instructive and they enrich the text, but they add considerable length as well as diffusing the focus from the hero's growth. For Paterson's purposes, simpler is better.

Sadly, however, this simplicity means that Paterson must sacrifice some of the most charming elements of the original. The German poem is much funnier and richer than the modern retelling, in part because of the complexity of Parzival's character, the dual meanings of words, and the presence of Wolfram as narrator. Paterson keeps only a hint of Parzival's youthful literalness, one of the most comic aspects of his character. In the medieval poem, before he leaves home in search of adventure Parzival's mother gives him instructions, telling him, among other things, to "beware of dark fords" (1961, 72). When the boy comes upon a brook that "a rooster could probably have crossed" (72), he goes miles out of his way rather than cross it because the "flowers and grass . . . made its stream so dark" (73)—an episode Paterson deletes. The episode sets up the next sequence of Parzival interpreting his mother's instructions literally, which Paterson includes in her version: Parzival takes a lady's ring and kisses her—forcibly—because his mother told him "wherever you can win a good woman's ring and greeting, take them . . . you must make haste to kiss her and clasp her tight in your embrace" (72). All of this literal interpretation of advice is an important element of the work, since it leads to Parzival's first failure to achieve the Grail. His teacher, Gurnemanz, cautions him not to ask too many questions. Gurnemanz's instructions are fitting for the chivalric world of Arthur's court, but when Parzival comes to the Grail Castle, a different set of rules apply: compassion, not courtesy, should guide him. Instead of asking the suffering Grail King a question that would indicate compassion and concern, Parzival remains silent, intent upon following Gurnemanz's instructions. By this point in the story, Parzival's literal understanding of the world and his simplicity have been well-established; they are, by necessity, less well-established in the modern retelling.

Paterson must also simplify language, referring for example to Munsalvaesche, the Grail Castle, as "The Wild Mountain." In the poem, the name has a double meaning, echoing both the words "savage" (or wild) and "salvation." The words indicate the castle's complex and confusing nature: although one may find salvation there, it is a dangerous land where "grave harm can befall a stranger" (1961, 136). Paterson simplifies this name and others, and she also chooses to delete Wolfram's comic asides. He complains to his patron that he needs more money, he compares himself to other poets, both real and imaginary, and he comments sagely on women and wine. In her endnote, however, Paterson tells the reader about her omissions, including Wolfram's asides, Sir Gawain, and Parzival's father.

What Paterson does *not* tell the reader is that she has also simplified the Grail itself. In her retelling, the Grail takes the form modern readers are accustomed to: the "sacred vessel" (51). In medieval literature, however, the Grail takes many other forms, its most curious in *Parzival*, where it is a green stone. The ceremony surrounding the Grail is complicated enough and it is clear why Paterson would choose to simplify this idea, but in some ways it's a shame that she didn't mention the Grail's form in her endnote, since readers are so often surprised and fascinated to learn that the medieval idea of the Grail was not necessarily the chalice we are familiar with from pre-Raphaelite paintings. Fortunately, for readers whose interest is piqued by Paterson's version of the tale, English translations of the entire poem are easily available, both in prose and in verse.

From retellings like Paterson's, Cadnum's borrowings, and other writers' incorporation of medieval literature within their novels, readers can not only become involved in a good story, they can also learn a little about the poetry and prose of the Middle Ages. Teachers might pair canonical texts such as *Beowulf* and *The Canterbury Tales* with contemporary novels such as those discussed here, in order to provide students with a gateway into the medieval era. The discrepancies in Temple's presentation of medieval life can be a jumping-off point for discussions of attitudes towards gender and class in the Middle Ages. Examining a short passage from the medieval and modern *Parzival*, or *Beowulf* as it is presented in Alder's novel, allows students to engage in close textual reading as well as in comparison. Comparison between the reactions Temple's characters have to a story from *The Canterbury Tales*, the students' own reactions, and the ways Chaucer's pilgrims respond can lead to a clearer understanding of some of the differences in attitudes that characterize modern and medieval society. However they are used, these texts within novels accord with the medieval ideal for literature: they both teach and delight.

Chapter Four

Saxons and Normans

English history and literature teachers often look to the Anglo-Saxon period as one worthy of study, even if students don't agree. *Beowulf* and the Norman Conquest of England still fill textbooks, if not always students' imaginations. Perhaps fiction can help students find this era, which teachers know to be exciting, a little more compelling. Four novelists who write about the end of Anglo-Saxon England, the Norman Conquest, and the transition from Saxon to Norman England tell their tales with a refreshing lack of didacticism. Eloise McGraw's *The Striped Ships* (1991) and Elizabeth Alder's *The King's Shadow* (1995) take place directly before or after the Conquest and introduce readers to customs both Anglo-Saxon and Norman. Readers also learn of the complicated political situation found in eleventh-century England. Although the Robin Hood legend has perpetuated a simplistic dichotomy by pitting innocent Saxons like Robin and Maid Marian against evil, oppressive Normans like Prince John, in reality the situation was as complex and ambiguous as the events surrounding the Conquest itself. We see some of the complexity of England's twelfth-century identity struggle in Rosemary Sutcliff's *The Witch's Brat* (1970), as well as in the political anarchy that provides the setting for Joan Elizabeth Goodman's *The Winter Hare* (1996). In this chapter, I introduce readers to the historical documents that play a large role in three of the novels. In addition, readers get some background on a particular medieval time and place: England in the eleventh and twelfth centuries.

The End of Anglo-Saxon England

The events of the year 1066 propelled English history towards a different course than it had followed in the five centuries since the Anglo-Saxons invaded England. But many of the actual events of that year and those directly preceding it are not well documented and are difficult to interpret. Relationships between England and Normandy in these years are confusing. For example, history isn't very clear about the relationship between King Harold Godwinson, the last English king before the Norman Conquest, and Duke William of Normandy, England's Conqueror. Here's what we do know: At the death of King Edward the Confessor in 1065, there were three claimants to the English throne—Harold Godwinson, William of Normandy, and Harold Hardrada, the king of Norway. None of these men was a direct descendent of the dead king. (The only direct descendent, Edgar the Aetheling, was apparently too young and weak to assume the throne.) It appears that both King Edward the Confessor and the king's council, known as the *witan*, named Harold Godwinson his successor. But the other two claimants were unhappy with this decision. First Harold Hardrada, allied with Harold's brother Tostig and the Northumbrian earls, attacked in the North. When the new king had defeated the Norwegian and Northumbrian armies, he returned south to face a new invader, Duke William, at Hastings. And there "at the hoary apple tree . . . King Harold was killed . . . and the French remained masters of the field, even as God granted it to them because of the sins of the people" (Whitelock 1961, 143).

These words appear in *The Anglo-Saxon Chronicle,* one of two important medieval documents discussed in this chapter that record the end of Anglo-Saxon England. The other is the Bayeux Tapestry. Two modern novels incorporate these historical documents into their own telling of the events leading up to and directly following the Norman Conquest. In *The King's Shadow,* Evyn, whom we met in Chapter Three singing verses from *The Song of Roland,* travels with Harold Godwinson in the years before Harold will die in battle at Duke William's hands. Because his tongue has been cut out, Evyn must find a different means to communicate, and he learns to read and write, becoming one of the people who records events in *The Anglo-Saxon Chronicle.* The novel ends in 1066, the year of the Conquest, the event that begins *The Striped Ships.* In McGraw's novel, Juliana tells of the coming of the Normans to coastal England and the subjugation she and other Anglo-Saxon people suffered after William won the Battle of Hastings. Juliana finds employment helping to embroider the Bayeux Tapestry, and she tells the tapestry's designer what she saw the day the striped ships came. Both McGraw and Alder retell history from the point of view of the losing side, and both invent lively, compelling protagonists who witness and interact with history in the making—and with the recording of that history. Both writers skillfully weave history lessons into their stories as they present historically accurate renderings of eleventh-century England.

The Anglo-Saxon Chronicle and The King's Shadow

The Anglo-Saxon Chronicle frames *The King's Shadow*. Not only does Evyn help write it, but each of the novel's chapters begins with an inscription either taken directly from the *Chronicle* or modeled on its prose. *The Anglo-Saxon Chronicle* differs from other medieval history-writing because, unlike other European annals, it was written in the vernacular, in English—the Old English of *Beowulf*—rather than in Latin. Most entries are short, from a line to a few paragraphs, and record events of a particular year. Most use a formulaic opening, which Alder adopts in her novel: For example, a *Chronicle* entry for the year 835 begins, "Her cuom micel sciphere," or "In this year a large ship-army came." The Anglo-Saxon word *her*, which begins so many of the *Chronicle* entries, literally means "here," but takes on the context of "In this year" or "At this time." Alder incorporates it into her chapter headings as "In this year," giving her prose a texture reminiscent of the *Chronicle*. She varies her chapter headings by breaking up sentences so that two consecutive chapter headings might complete a sentence: "1064: In this year a storm left Earl Harold shipwrecked. . . . " (112) is followed by a chapter headed, "1064: . . . and he and his men spent many weeks at the Norman court" (126). (In reality, none of the surviving versions of the chronicle has an entry for the year 1064.) Alder's use of chronicle style in the headings of the novel accustoms readers to it so that by the end of the novel, when Evyn begins to record history as he saw it happen during the years 1063–66 by writing entries in the *Anglo-Saxon Chronicle*, the passages that begin "In this year" come as no surprise. Readers recognize what Evyn is writing and Alder is able to quote sections of the *Chronicle* almost verbatim in her novel without them seeming out of place

> 1065 In this year, after the feast of Michaelmas, the Northumbrians united to outlaw Tostig, their Earl. They slew his housecarls, took his weapons, and carried off his gold and silver. They sent for Morcar, son of Earl Alfgar, and chose him to be their Earl. (258)

Alder must invent, summarize, and conflate some passages in order to fit the needs of her novel (for example, adding an entry for the year 1064), but where she can, she quotes directly.

Different versions of the *Chronicle* were kept and recorded by different monasteries, so it is fitting that Evyn writes of events he knows from his place in the monastery at Athelney. Evyn, however, is not a monk, like the usual recorders. Seven manuscripts of the *Chronicle* survive today, and the events they record diverge from each other at times, reflecting local happenings as well as ones of national character.

The *Peterborough Chronicle*, which will be discussed below, is famous for being continuously recorded through the year 1154 (other chronicles end anywhere from 977 to 1080). All but two of the manuscripts are kept in the British Library in London. The others are in libraries in Oxford and Cambridge. Although the style of the *Chronicle* is usually simple prose, poems such as "The Battle of Brunanburh," mentioned in Chapter Three, are included as well. This poem, which recounts an English victory over northern invaders, is the entry for the year 937 in four manuscripts of *The Anglo-Saxon Chronicle*. In *The King's Shadow,* a storyteller recites the poem in Lady Ealdgyth's hall (49)—reminding Evyn of his own blighted desire to be a storyteller.

Evyn's social status increases dramatically throughout the novel. While Juliana, in *The Striped Ships*, is reduced from noble to slave, Evyn starts life as a Welsh serf, then becomes a slave to the Anglo-Saxons, and finally, is adopted into the Anglo-Saxon nobility, when, near the end of the book, King Harold makes Evyn his foster son. Readers might be surprised to learn that slaves were common in England and on the continent during the Anglo-Saxon period. Many of the people who became slaves were on the losing side of a battle, as is Juliana when she becomes a slave to the Normans. Evyn is from Wales and, like him, many of the Anglo-Saxon slaves were of Celtic stock, and known, like Evyn, for their dark hair. In Anglo-Saxon poetry, dark hair, as opposed to the fair hair common to Anglo-Saxons, implies a lower status (Pelteret 1995, 52). In fact, the word Welsh (*wealh* in Anglo-Saxon) could mean slave or foreigner, as well as Welsh. (In their own language, the Welsh, who lived in Britain long before the Anglo-Saxons arrived, call themselves *Y Cymry* and their land *Cymru*.)

When Evyn becomes a slave, he is forced to wear an iron neck ring—something that probably wouldn't have happened in reality. Although slaves were sometimes punished by being placed in wrist or ankle irons (Pelteret 1995, 58), there seems to be no evidence for the "thrall ring" that Evyn wears. In fact, the need to have witnesses at any manumission in order to "ensure that those responsible for local law-keeping were aware that someone who had just been freed was moving about the district legally" (Pelteret 1995, 148) implies that no physical symbol marked one as a slave.

Alder's reliance on historical events to shape her narrative is impressive, as is her knowledge of Anglo-Saxon culture. Many of the concepts she includes are standard parts of life in Anglo-Saxon England: wergild, earls, thanes and churls, small fighting forces made up of housecarls, and large armies made up of all men over the age of sixteen. Early in the book, for example, we read about the wergild (literally, man-price) that Evyn's uncle must pay for killing another man.

The concept was part of Anglo-Saxon law, and a person's price was dependent on social status. Alder's portrayal of Lady Ealdgyth's great hall and the estate is also accurate, according to what we know of how the Anglo-Saxons lived. The housecarls, or men of high social status who live, travel, and fight with Earl Harold, are recorded in historical accounts, as is the great peasant army known as the *fyrd*.

Earls and thanes are men of higher classes in Anglo-Saxon society, and churls are the lower classes. Earls, whose wergild was three times that of churls, were directly below the king in status. They governed the English shires and commanded each shire's *fyrd*. In the time just before the Norman Conquest, the shires had been consolidated into four main regions, each governed by an earl. This is why, in *The King's Shadow*, Harold is referred to as the Earl of Wessex, and his brother Tostig as the Earl of Northumbria. After the Conquest, William changed the word "earl" to "count," and "shire" to "county," in order to make England more like Normandy, although in practice, the title "earl" was still used, and it was formally reestablished in the fifteenth century, "though an earl's wife is still styled a 'countess'" (Boulton 1998, 261).

Not as high as the earl, but still a nobleman, is the thane (spelled *thegn* in Old English). In *The Striped Ships*, Juliana's father is a thane. Below the thane is the churl, the large peasant class. For us, the word "churl" has a negative connotation, but in Anglo-Saxon England, a churl (*ceorl*) was a free man who generally owned the land he farmed. There were other gradations in class, and there were those who didn't fit easily into any of these categories, such as monks and merchants. Below them all were the slaves.

Alder's portrayal of Anglo-Saxon society is remarkably accurate. Nevertheless, some of her story is hard to believe. That Harold would take pity on a tongueless slave, we might accept. But that Harold would elevate that boy to the status of squire, particularly when communication is so difficult between the two of them, strains credulity. The squire was the warrior's third hand and fast communication was vital. A fighting man such as Harold, who spent a great deal of his time putting down rebellions or patrolling borders, would have need of a squire who could communicate quickly and easily on horseback. Nor is it easy to believe that a noble lady would ask a slave to serve as a page at an important dinner, as Lady Ealdgyth does with Evyn. Pages were sons of nobility, and it would have been insulting to ask them to work alongside a slave, and a Welsh one, at that. During a tense political situation, tenuous loyalties needed to be nurtured, and it simply wouldn't have been worth it for Ealdgyth to insult a young man who might carry the story home to his noble father. But for the sake of the plot, the novelist must take some liberties, and Alder is careful not to take too many liberties with her portrayal of Anglo-Saxon England.

The Bayeux Tapestry and *The Striped Ships*

Although the Bayeux Tapestry was made within a generation of the Battle of Hastings, scholars are still unsure which side, Norman or Saxon, was responsible for its construction. Like any novelist, Eloise McGraw has had to invent some facts—where the work was made, who made it and why, for example—but she keeps her conjectures very close to what we know of the tapestry. First of all, its name is a misnomer: the work is embroidery, not tapestry, and McGraw shows both men and women working as embroiderers (which is consistent with scholarly opinion). Secondly, the work's patron is Bishop Odo of Bayeux (in Normandy), yet the embroidering takes place in Canterbury, England—both in McGraw's version and according to what historians believe. It may, then, be both a Norman and a Saxon work. As a monk in the workroom says to Juliana, the determined heroine of *The Striped Ships*, "it must not tell only a Norman truth" (171). And, as J. Bard McNulty observes, many scholars who look for evidence of the work being purely Norman or purely Saxon forget that "there may have been, following the Conquest, various Norman as well as various Saxon views of the event" (1998, 110).

The Tapestry, which is visible to the public at a museum dedicated to it in Bayeux, France, and in several facsimiles, records, in both images and in writing, events from 1064–1066. It begins with Harold's trip to Normandy, discussed in the next section, and ends with the Battle of Hastings, although some of the end of the embroidery may have been lost. The inscriptions above the pictures are in Latin; they identify characters and briefly describe events in phrases such as these: "Here the horses leave the boats" and "Here were killed Leofwine and Gyrth, the brothers of King Harold" or "Here is Duke William" (Wilson 1985, 173). (Readers might notice the similarity to the simple prose style of *The Anglo-Saxon Chronicle*, although the Tapestry's inscriptions are in Latin and begin with the word *Hic*, not the Old English *Her*. Both words, in this context, can be translated "Here.") David M. Wilson's facsimile, *The Bayeux Tapestry* (1985), provides not only color photos of the entire tapestry, but also transcriptions and translations of the Latin inscriptions, a commentary on the action in each scene, and a discussion of the story and art. When you think of the Tapestry, picture not a heavy rectangular wall-hanging meant to keep out drafts in medieval castles, like the Unicorn Tapestries. Instead, think of a very long, very thin strip of linen, not quite two feet high, but seventy-six yards long, three quarters as long as a football field. On it are embroidered many narrative pictures in rusty orange and mustardy yellow, blue-green, and black.

The striped ships of McGraw's title refer to the long ships with animal-headed prows, one large sail, and horizontal stripes of orange, dark green, and mustard that appear in the scenes of Harold's trip to Normandy as well as, later, in the pictures of Norman invaders crossing the English Channel. As Harold wades barefoot out to his ship, he tucks his tunic up around his waist with one hand while his hawk sits on his other hand. A man follows him, tunic likewise tucked, carrying two dogs.

William's ships, like Harold's, are filled with warriors and lined at the top with the warriors' tear-drop shaped shields. In scenes directly preceding William's Channel crossing, men load the ships with spears and helmets, mail shirts, axes, and swords, in addition to food and other supplies in barrels and bags. Norman men are distinguished from the English by their hair styles: Normans wear the backs of their heads shaved, while the English sport jaunty mustaches.

A favorite game amongst Bayeux Tapestry observers is interpreting the scenes in the borders, which, like marginal decorations in many illuminated manuscripts, tell little stories. Many have tried to find hidden Saxon symbols and meanings—English commentaries on the Norman invaders—within the borders. These scenes are notoriously difficult to interpret; after one scholar demonstrated that some of them illustrate fables from Aesop, others tried without much success to find Aesop elsewhere in the pictures. The marginal images are diverse, like the images in the margins of psalters and other manuscripts. Some of the scenes depict plowing and hunting, others show animals, both ordinary and fabulous, rams and roosters as well as centaurs and dragons. Some pictures are bawdy. Why is that naked man with an erect penis crouching in the margin directly below the picture of a woman? In fact, what are *all* those naked men and women doing in the margins? We may never know. McGraw capitalizes on the ambiguity of the marginal images by allowing some of them to tell Juliana's story: the monk who designs the pictures includes scenes of carnage in the borders after Juliana haltingly tells what happened to her community when the Normans landed.

When we look back at events like the Norman Conquest from the distance of centuries, it's tempting to oversimplify and to break complex relationships into easy dichotomies. McGraw refuses to do that in *The Striped Ships*. Although Juliana tries to divide her society into two groups, Normans and Saxons, McGraw demonstrates the weakness of Juliana's attempt. There was plenty of contact between Normandy and England before the Conquest, particularly during the reign of King Edward the Confessor (1042–1066). According to Frank Barlow (1970), King Edward and his family "probably spoke no English" (217), preferring French, instead. Not all English people hated Normans. While some Saxons wanted nothing but to kill Normans, others, like Juliana's mother, use their Norman connections to save themselves and live comfortably. Juliana's uncle, who lives in Winchester, is Norman. After the battle and the death of Juliana's father, her mother flees to her Norman brother-in-law and eventually marries a Norman baron. With her simplistic view of the world, Juliana can accept neither her uncle nor her mother's alliance with him. She also believes that Saxons will look out for other Saxons, only becoming disabused of this idea when, to her dismay, Saxon robbers steal her food and cloak.

For some people in England, the Conquest brings little change: Juliana realizes that because of his isolation, a hermit she meets in the forest is unaware of the tumultuous events England has experienced. For her younger brother, Wulfric, the Conquest brings about immediate hardship, but he never loses sight of his dream to be a *scriptor*, or scribe in a monastery. Although the Saxon abbots and priors might be replaced with Norman ones, monasteries still need boys to be novices, and once Wulfric enters the monastery, his life is much the same as it would have been had the striped ships never sailed for England's shores.

For Juliana, however, life changes drastically. Formerly a cosseted thane's daughter, a member of the nobility who has slaves and servants to do her bidding, Juliana becomes a slave to the Normans. She finds herself working alongside her own former slave, Rhonwen, a Welsh girl. For Rhonwen, the Conquest is an opportunity, not a tragedy. For her it matters not whether she is slave to an Anglo-Saxon or a Norman lord, and after the Battle of Hastings, she finds her way to relative wealth and comfort, and more importantly, freedom from slavery, by becoming the mistress of a Norman knight whose wife lives in Normandy. Juliana wants to believe that Rhonwen's life was better in Juliana's father's house, but Rhonwen tells her that a slave is a slave, whether the master be Norman or Saxon. As Juliana struggles to accept these truths, she also struggles to find a place in her strange new world. Eventually she finds work and a place to live, but she will never again enjoy her earlier social status.

Juliana's loss of social status is more believable than Evyn's rise from slave to noble. No deus ex machina device saves Juliana from her fate; instead, she finds her own way in the harsh world in which she has found herself. That she would not live with her mother is made easier to accept by her finding of another family, one she was formerly betrothed into, to take her in. By situating her heroine in a time of enormous social unrest and change, McGraw avoids the problem so many writers encounter of giving a female character in the medieval period too much power and control over her own life. Like Alder, McGraw responsibly incorporates research about late Anglo-Saxon and early Anglo-Norman culture into her novel. She reveals much about monasteries and religious ceremonies as well as about Anglo-Saxon and Norman clothing, architecture, and food. And like Alder, McGraw creates a character who the reader likes and roots for as her fortunes change.

Historical Ambiguity in
The King's Shadow and *The Striped Ships*

The ambiguity of Harold Godwinson's relationship to Duke William in the years before the Conquest plays a large role in both *The King's Shadow* and *The Striped Ships*. According to both the Bayeux Tapestry and Norman chronicles, Harold visited Normandy and took an oath to William. However, exactly why Harold took either the journey or the oath is unclear. Nor is it clear exactly what the oath decreed. The Bayeux Tapestry text is sparse, with only two inscriptions about this event: "Here William came to Bayeux" and "Where Harold made an oath to Duke William" (Wilson 1985, 172). Later Norman versions of Harold's trip, which are necessarily propagandistic, say that Harold came to Normandy strictly to swear an oath of allegiance to William. *The Anglo-Saxon Chronicle* records nothing for the year 1064, the year Harold visited Normandy. It's this tangle of events that novelists have to unravel for their stories, deciding on one thread and following it to its logical end.

For McGraw, the oath is a question Juliana raises over and over again, worrying it the way a dog worries a bone. Juliana wants Harold to be perfect and to have done no wrong. A discussion with her older brother Sweyn leads her to understand that even kings have foibles and that perhaps the king made an error. He tells her that Harold swore his fealty to William on holy relics, a very solemn vow. "William may have tricked him. But he swore," Sweyn says (87). Later, Juliana has a similar conversation with a Norman monk, the designer of the Bayeux Tapestry, whose account of Harold's oath agrees with Sweyn's. Juliana is concerned that her hero, the dead king, may have broken his oath. Like Sweyn, the monk allows for the possibility that Harold might have been tricked. And like Sweyn, he reminds her that although kings have human flaws, they can be heroes nonetheless (182–3). McGraw's version of history is as complex and tangled as the embroidery threads that Juliana winds.

Alder's Harold, on the other hand, comes as close to perfection as Juliana would have him be. Alder paints history in broad strokes, portraying Harold as a man whose "courage and selflessness set him apart" (147). He is a magnanimous hero to Duke William's base and cruel coward. The entire episode leading up to the oath appears in *The King's Shadow:* Harold's shipwreck on Norman shores, his capture by Count Guy, William's rescuing Harold from Guy and treating him royally, even taking him to a battle against rebels in Brittany. Although he swears an oath of fealty to William, he is clearly tricked into doing so in order to save himself and his men. Unwilling to allow any question of Harold's character, the narrator tells us that "Although this was a coerced oath and not legally binding, Harold had no way to prove that it was an un-willing pledge without endangering all his men" (134). Like Juliana, Alder wants Harold to be more than human, and in this way her novel is less convincing than McGraw's.

Juliana and Evyn are the only surviving witnesses to many of the events their histories record. Evyn writes what he knows in *The Anglo-Saxon Chronicle* and Juliana tells the tapestry designer what she has seen so that he can record it in pictures. Both texts, the written and pictor-ial ones, are ambiguous, and both novelists are forced to decide how to interpret some of the events, just as they must make decisions about how to portray daily life in Anglo-Saxon England. Since so much of the literature from the Anglo-Saxon period was written by monks and only incidentally describes the homely, everyday events so essential to novelists, neither Alder nor McGraw had much to draw on. However, they have used what little we do know responsibly, portraying the late Anglo-Saxon world as one divided by classes, served by slaves, and bound by loyalty to one's lord.

From Anglo-Saxon to Anglo-Norman

The Norman Invasion of England brought about many changes, cul-tural and linguistic, some of which are reflected in *The Striped Ships*. Juliana hears Norman French spoken around her and she must learn to live by Norman rules. Forty years later, when Anglo-Saxon England is still part of living memory, the transition continues. We see it in Rose-mary Sutcliff's *The Witch's Brat* (1970) when characters either speak mutually unintelligible Saxon or Norman French. Another forty years pass before the setting of Joan Elizabeth Goodman's *The Winter Hare* (1996), which takes place in a turbulent, but thoroughly Anglo-Norman world of the aristocracy, where only a hint of the Anglo-Saxon past still remains.

William the Conqueror brought with him to England not only his language, but many of his friends, whom he set in high places. Out with the English church authorities, in with the Norman. Out with the English earls, in with the Norman counts, whom William married to many a widow whose husband had died fighting alongside Harold. Forcing the widows to marry Norman counts put large parcels of English land into the hands of Norman nobility, since Anglo-Saxon women, particularly widows, could be major landholders. The replacement of abbots meant that monasteries, which had considerable political power, would be loyal to the new king. Saxon serfs chafed under some of William's new laws, such as the idea of the Royal Forest, which prohib-ited them from not only hunting, but also cutting trees and pasturing animals in most of England's still-vast forests. According to *The Anglo-Saxon Chronicle,* William "loved the stags as if he were their father," implying that deer were more valuable than people. "The harsh reality of that law," writes Charles Young, "provided the background for a fictional Robin Hood transmitted to future generations through popular ballads" (1998, 301).

A remarkable and fascinating document from William's reign is Domesday Book, the survey of his property that William ordered in 1085—and by property, he meant farms and forests, pigs, people, and pastures, everything in all of England. According to one of the Anglo-Saxon chroniclers,

> so very thoroughly did he have the kingdom investigated that there was not a single [piece of land] . . . or even (it is shameful to record but did not seem shameful to him to do), one ox or one cow or one pig that was omitted from his record; and all these records were afterward brought to him. (Fleming 1998, 241)

The Domesday Book entries, which still survive, were written in Latin and give us details about "45,000 landholdings across the kingdom," and what they were like in both 1066 and in 1086—and therefore what changes the Conquest wrought on them (Fleming 1998, 241).

The changes to England included the importation of French into the country, although it was only used by the nobility. Ever tried to learn a second language? William the Conqueror tried with English when he was forty-three, but gave up—it was too hard, and besides, he was busy. His successors William II and Henry I both spent much of their lives in Normandy, where they were dukes. They might have known some English, but it is clear that the kingdom still used two languages, French for the aristocracy and English for everyone else. In the 150 years following the Conquest, Norman French became the language of the courts, of government, and of the church (along with Latin). By 1204, however, the conflict between King John of England and King Philip of France meant that the Norman nobility had to choose between being completely English or completely French, once again separating the two nations and their languages.

The Witch's Brat

The Witch's Brat, which takes place during the reign of Henry I, is one of the three novels Rosemary Sutcliff sets in Norman England. The other two are set slightly before or after *The Witch's Brat: The Shield Ring* (1956) during the reign of William the Conqueror's successor, William Rufus, and *Knight's Fee* (1960) around the year 1100, during the very beginning of the reign of William Rufus's successor, Henry I. Miriam

Youngerman Miller (1994) praises Sutcliff's "linguistic sophistication" (27) in *The Shield Ring*, in which characters use language in authentic ways, speaking "Old English, Anglo-Norwegian, and Norman French" (26). *Knight's Fee* fares not nearly as well in Miller's analysis: "Sutcliff handles the major linguistic issue of the period, the relationship of the superstratum language French and the substratum language English, by denying that it exists" (27). Instead, Sutcliff dismisses the "problems deriving from the co-existence of French- and English-speakers in Norman England" (28). *The Witch's Brat* is written for a younger audience and thus is less complicated in plot as well as in language, although Miller takes Sutcliff to task for inappropriately using "nonstandard dialect as an indication of lower class status" (29): since Lovel, the main character, is a serf, his speech early in the novel should be as non-standard as that of Nick Redpoll, a lower-class character who appears in the end of the book, she argues.

Despite Miller's dissatisfaction, *The Witch's Brat* is well worth reading. Sutcliff lovingly pieces together England as it might have been under King Henry I. Her scholarship informs all of her novels, giving her the details to make her setting as complex as her characters. The Benedictine monastery near Winchester bustles with activity because when the king holds court at Winchester, travelers lodge at the monastery. But it's more complicated than that: the poor and pilgrims stay in one place where the hospitaller looks after them, knights and merchants get better lodgings and better service, while nobles lodge with the abbot himself. In one or two chapters, Sutcliff plans and peoples her monastery, giving readers the feeling that she has spent some time in an early twelfth-century minster. Details, details, that's how she does it, but details woven into the story, not added to it in textbook manner.

The same kinds of details enhance the setting for the second part of the book, the new St. Bartholomew's priory and hospital, just outside of London. It's under construction during the novel, but even half-finished stones are fully realized, and even minor characters fully constructed.

The novel covers Lovel's life from his early teens to his early twenties. During that time he matures from a frightened, abused boy to a self-assured healer, a valuable member of first the monastery and later, the hospital. His physical handicaps, a hunched shoulder that gets him scorned and stoned and called "Humpy" early in his life, and a weak, twisted leg, are liabilities that become assets in the end, when a boy trusts Lovel's healing hands because of his physical deformities.

Like Ursula in *There Will Be Wolves* and Gabrielle in *Dove and Sword*, Lovel early on identifies himself as a healer. Like Ursula, he attends a dog with a broken leg before he begins to heal humans. Like Gabrielle, he understands the broken leg not from reading about it in a book (as Ursula does) but from feeling the bones and knowing what they should feel like. Lovel is interested in the herbal, the manuscript about plants, that he sees in the monastery library, and his interest in it leads another monk not only to teach him to read, but to get him a job in the monastery herb garden and infirmary. Because it is so many-faceted, not just book-centered, Lovel's medical education seems authentic. By helping his grandmother gather and prepare herbs, by watching her work with those sick of body and of heart, Lovel is introduced to the healing arts. By tending the monastery's herb garden, helping to prepare the herbs, and serving in the infirmary—which sometimes means simply sitting with a dying monk—Lovel becomes a healer, one who, as a young man, is competent enough to join the hospital established by the king's minstrel.

From the first time he meets him, Lovel is drawn to the historical figure Rahere, King Henry I's jongleur. Juggling and singing and acting the fool become tedious for Rahere, who becomes an Augustinian canon and founds the hospital. When he needs a trained healer to join him in this new work, he whistles and Lovel comes limping from Winchester to London, where he finds both purpose and home.

The Winter Hare

A leap of forty years and a focus on the nobility make the world of *The Winter Hare* distinctly different from that of *The Witch's Brat*. Like *The King's Shadow*, the novel is based on *The Anglo-Saxon Chronicle*, but the worlds the two books represent are far apart. Gone from the upper-classes is much in the way of the Anglo-Saxon past. These are Norman knights, whose exploits are detailed in *The Peterborough Chronicle*, which is famous for having been kept until 1153, far later than the other versions of the *Chronicle*. The events from the years 1137–1141 are the ones Joan Elizabeth Goodman uses in *The Winter Hare* as she tells the story of Will Belet, an Anglo-Norman youth who longs to be a knight. Will is part of the distinctly feudal society that England had become in the century after the Norman Conquest, and Norman French surnames are more common than Anglo-Saxon ones in Will's world, his own—Belet—among them. Will serves Sir Aubrey de Vere, for example, and Ranulf d'Artois is a knight of Will's father's.

Goodman takes a hands-off approach to her source, mentioning it only in her Author's Note and keeping her focus on her invented character, Will, and his tribulations. Up until the year 1121, *The Peterborough Chronicle* is a copy of an older manuscript; beginning in 1121 the entries are new to this chronicle. Into the copy of the pre-1121 material, the Peterborough scribe inserted "entries for various years" as well as "pseudo-charters, distinguished by their language as belonging to the twelfth century, and by their content as inserted at Peterborough" (Bennett and Smithers 1968, 201). Here was a cheap way to gain lands for your monastery: insert a faked charter into an official document!

The chronicle entries from 1132 to 1155 seem to have been made all at one time. They differ from the earlier versions of *The Anglo-Saxon Chronicle* because they use a very personal first-person voice. This has led some scholars to speculate that we are hearing the voice of an old monk telling the story of events he witnessed (Bennett and Smithers 1968, 202). And those events are horrible. The long chronicle entry for 1137 details, with strong disapproval, what happened during King Stephen's reign, the setting for *The Winter Hare*. "I ne can ne I ne mai tellen alle þe wunder ne alle þe pines ðat hi diden wrecce men on þis land, and ðat lastede þa xix wintre wile Stephne was king, and æure it was uuerse and uuerse" the chronicler writes (Bennett and Smithers 1968, 208): I neither know nor am able to tell all the atrocities nor all the sufferings that they did to wretched men in this land, and that lasted nineteen years while Stephen was king, and always it was worse and worse. The chronicler calls King Stephen a fool and describes in gruesome detail the tortures Stephen and his men inflict on both men and women. He tells of the unfair taxes, the robbing and burning of villages, the misery and starvation of the poor.

Although this is Will Belet's world in *The Winter Hare*, Will is sheltered from the atrocities because he is a member of the nobility who has grown up on an out-of-the-way estate. Once he moves to Oxford to be a page at the Earl of Oxford's court, he is closer to the center of action. He learns first-hand the horror of battle and siege, but the sufferings of the peasantry are of little interest to him, since he spends his time among his social peers, cut off from the lower classes by castle walls and the walls of class distinctions. He does briefly think about their inability to feed themselves during times of scarcity because they can't hunt in the Royal Forest. But Will has his own troubles: he is too small to be a good knight, according to all the other knights. And worse yet, he and his older brother are in danger of losing their lives because the powerful Earl of Oxford covets their father's estate for his own son. Will finds himself protecting his older brother, who is twice wounded under suspicious circumstances. Like Lovel in *The Witch's Brat*, Will's medical knowledge earns him the respect of men who formerly scorned him because of his size. Will learns about healing in a realistic way, from watching and helping his mother, not from spending his days reading books.

Like the presentation of medical education, the portrayal of women is generally historically accurate. It is to Goodman's credit that in the end of the book, Will's friend Edith does not escape her arranged marriage to a much older knight. Both Will and the reader harbor expectations that Edith might marry Will, but he is the youngest son of a knight, and she the youngest daughter of another. As Edith says, "my portion is small" (249); so is Will's. Edith needs to marry into wealth, which is what her parents have arranged for her. Although her parents are fond of Will, they are also practical, and Edith shows sad acceptance of her situation. Will accepts it, too, knowing how little material wealth he has to offer Edith. And anyway, he has plenty of adventure ahead of him. At the end of the novel, he pledges himself to serve young Henry Plantagenet, who still has a kingdom to gain.

The complex political situation of these years, with a usurping king, two queens named Matilda (one married to the king, the other his cousin and the rightful heir to the throne), and many nobles with shifting loyalties, lies behind Will's story but is not woven into it in the detailed way that Anglo-Saxon history is a part of *The King's Shadow*. At the end of her novel, Goodman capitalizes on a single, thrilling event from *The Peterborough Chronicle*. When King Stephen besieges the tower Empress Matilda is in, "she was let down at night from the tower with ropes, and she stole out and fled and went on foot to Wallingford" (Whitelock 1961, 202). Will not only helps Matilda to escape, he teaches her to ice skate so that she can skate her way to freedom down the frozen Thames, a conceivable if unlikely invention on Goodman's part.

The Winter Hare hardly gives readers a clear picture of political events, except by demonstrating how confusing those events were. Readers will, however, see some generic medieval customs, such as Twelfth Night celebrations. The richness of detail and characterization that distinguish *The Witch's Brat, The King's Shadow,* and *The Striped Ships* is not in evidence here. Nor are Anglo-Saxon customs and resentments against the Normans, so much a part of *The Striped Ships*—nor should they be for an Anglo-Norman boy living eighty years after the Conquest. Soon Normandy and England will again be divided, but England will never go back to being Anglo-Saxon. The intervening century has brought large-scale changes in culture and language that will stay with England. A few names are all that remain of the Anglo-Saxons in Will Belet's world.

Despite the survival of documents about the end of Saxon England and the beginning of the Norman era, ambiguity pervades our understanding of them. While McGraw uses this ambiguity to her advantage, enriching her novel by her portrayal of Juliana's desire to oversimplify, Alder herself oversimplifies Saxon heroes and Norman villains. All of the novelists discussed here present a dynamic period in which cultural diversity was an issue, and for the most part, they do so admirably. Their characters' reactions to others are neither contrived nor false: Juliana feels anger towards the conquering Normans, about whom she knows little but assumes much, and Evyn's understanding of events around him is textured and nuanced. Sutcliff's Lovel lacks our perspective on his historical period, remarking only on what he sees before him, not on what readers know from hindsight. And Will Belet fits into his class, the Anglo-Norman aristocracy of twelfth-century England, with no anachronistic thoughts of the Anglo-Saxons who came before him. Despite differences in the quality of their novels, all of these writers use historical documents and facts responsibly, remaining true to the past.

Chapter Five

Saints and Sinners
Historical Figures Fictionalized

When novelists present historical figures, who gets to tell the story—the historical figure? An invented character? And what of the novelists? Their decisions help to determine how readers perceive the characters. The novelists themselves may try to keep their own opinions about the characters hidden, but often readers can discern the novelists' own prejudices for or against the historical personage. In the same way, the authors' feelings about such issues as gender and class may be revealed, particularly when they people their novels with historically inaccurate characters. Some of the best portrayals show us historical characters within an authentic social milieu, and reveal these characters as complex humans with faults as well as admirable qualities, torn by vanity, by pride, even by their desire to do good. After all, even saints are sometimes sinners.

The perspective both author and characters take helps shape readers' views of historical characters and events. Both *The Striped Ships* and *The King's Shadow*, discussed in Chapter Four, compel readers to dislike Normans in favor of the English, to dislike William in favor of Harold. The historical documents that survive don't tell us much about their personalities, so the writers are free to invent. The scene shifts, however, with later historical figures like Peter Abelard, Joan of Arc, and Saint Francis of Assisi, about whom we know a great deal. Abelard left not only his scholarly writings to us, many of his letters to and from his lover, Heloise, also survive, as does his autobiography, *The History of My Misfortunes*. We have many of Francis's own writings, as well as accounts of his life by his contemporaries. Likewise with Joan of Arc. The transcripts of Joan's trial for heresy, as well as the posthumous hearing that acquitted her of heresy, in which the inhabitants of her village were interviewed, survive to give us a great deal of information about her life and her personality. In some ways, this wealth of information can fetter the novelist, rendering her less free to invent as she writes. The invention of characters to tell the story of the historical person allows writers to comment on the public figures. This is the case with Gabrielle, who narrates Nancy Garden's *Dove and Sword: A Novel of Joan of Arc* (1995), who I compare to Barbara Dana's Joan, who narrates her own tale in *Young Joan* (1991). Sometimes the invention of a protagonist leads the writer into dangerous territory, giving us a character with whom the author identifies, who comments on medieval events and attitudes with modern sensibilities, as does Ricca in Scott O'Dell's novel of Francis of Assisi, *The Road to Damietta* (1985). The most successful historical fiction allows readers to identify with the narrator, but at the same time, keeps the narrator's attitudes appropriate to the time period, as we see in Gloria Skurzynski's carefully researched novel, *Spider's Voice* (1999).

Abelard and Heloise in *Spider's Voice*

When we leap across the Channel from the Anglo-Norman England of *The Winter Hare* to Continental Europe during the twelfth century, we get a glimpse of life in an era when universities were just coming into being, an age sometimes called the Twelfth-Century Renaissance because the classical writers of Greece and particularly Rome were so highly valued. A look at the lives of Abelard and Heloise, the famous, doomed lovers of twelfth-century France, shows us much about education during the Romanesque period. Abelard, who was ten or twenty years older than Heloise, was employed by her uncle, in whose house she was raised, as her tutor. When Abelard met her, Heloise was already renowned for her knowledge of Latin. In fact, she was considered the most educated woman in Europe.

Abelard himself was also very well-educated in Latin language and literature. As his father's first-born son, he could have become a knight and inherited his father's lands, but he chose instead to pursue his education. In the Middle Ages, that meant pursuing a career in the church. A scholar was mainly a student of theology, and Abelard lectured to large groups of university students on the steps of Notre Dame cathedral in Paris about the Bible and the biblical commentaries written by the church fathers, such as Augustine and Jerome. It's here in Paris that Spider, the young mute boy who narrates Gloria Skurzynski's *Spider's Voice*, first sees his hero, Abelard. One of the two stories Spider tells throughout the novel is the tale of Abelard's affair with Heloise.

(Skurzynski uses the name Eloise because in French the initial H would not have been pronounced.)

We don't know who Heloise's parents were, but her uncle, Canon Fulbert, a church official, raised her. As a child she was educated in a convent, but when she was probably in her teens, and after she had learned everything she could from the nuns, she returned to her uncle's household. Fulbert liked having his niece know so much and he hired the already-famous teacher, Peter Abelard, to tutor her privately. Fulbert gave Abelard the same freedom with Heloise that any teacher would have had with a schoolboy—he could beat her as often as necessary to improve her learning. Although this sounds shocking to us, beatings went hand-in-hand with literacy and education, as the twelfth-century monk Guibert of Nogent makes clear in his memoir (Archambault 1996). Time and again Guibert refers to the beatings his tutor gave him. Every evening his mother asks him whether or not he "had been beaten that day" in school, and one day Guibert says she is upset to see that "my little arms were black and blue, and that the skin on my poor back was swollen all over from the canings I had received" (20). Boys and young men, however, were the usual recipients of the beatings, since girls rarely received such an extensive education as Heloise did. Her learning made Heloise like a museum piece: who was there for her to talk to about all the things she knew, except male clerics, who weren't supposed to spend their time with women? She didn't want to become a nun, even though a convent would have been a place where her education was more acceptable. Although she eventually entered a convent and become a very respected abbess, she did so against her will. Heloise never thought becoming a nun was the right thing for her to do because throughout her life she remained devoted to her earthly lover, Abelard, not to God.

All of the education both Heloise and Abelard received was in Latin. Almost all writing in Europe at this time was in Latin, and to be literate meant to read and write in Latin. Only in England was there a tradition of writing in vernacular languages. However, during Abelard's lifetime and in his home province, the troubadour tradition began. The troubadours composed in vernacular Romance languages like Occitan, Provençal, and French. Had he not been so good at Latin, Peter Abelard might have joined the court of the first troubadour, Count William IX of Poitou (Clanchy 1997, 53). Instead, Abelard opted for a clerical career. He became famous as a teacher and a scholar, not just a lover. His religious writings, especially *Sic et Non*, or *Yes and No*, were both famous and controversial, causing him at one point to be imprisoned for heresy. The problem with his work, and the reason it was controversial, was that Abelard found what seemed to be contradictory statements about Christian theology in the writings of church authorities. He collected them side by side with the intention that his students would use reason to resolve the apparent discrepancies. He was confident that discrepancies would be resolved: after all, hadn't "God created an ordered and rational universe"? (Clanchy 1997, 7). Abelard's enemies, particularly St. Bernard, believed that theological mysteries should not be exposed the way Abelard was revealing them. Michael Clanchy describes medieval Christianity this way:

> The 'faith of the simple' was preserved as a mystery by preventing lay people getting too close to the altars or seeing the miraculous shrines of the saints other than in the flickering light of candles. Even when sunlight was let into churches through stained glass windows . . . the new light did not make everything clear. It was even more ethereal than candles, as it dimmed and brightened with the seasons and the time of day, as if God Himself was ringing the changes. (1997, 8)

Throughout his life, Abelard battled with other churchmen about the proper ways to understand Christianity. Even when his books were ordered to be burned for heresy, his students copied them and preserved them, making him even more famous as a thinker.

Heloise, on the other hand, became famous only as a writer of love letters, despite her brilliance in Latin and in theology, because there was no place for women in the intellectual debates of male scholars. According to Clanchy, the "silencing of Heloise . . . was a prelude to the silencing of academic women as a class for the next eight centuries" (46). Heloise understood the intellectual debates and discussed them with Abelard, but she could not participate in them publicly. Had she written theological treatises the way Abelard did, no one would have read her work. Even in the nineteenth century, women writers took male pseudonyms in order to bypass this gender barrier, but in the twelfth century matters were much worse for women who wanted to live the life of the mind. Heloise probably influenced Abelard's writing, since her knowledge of "ancient philosophy and classical literature" was deeper than his (169). In some ways, according to Clanchy, Heloise "set the agenda which Abelard addressed in his theological writings" and she "expressed" some of the ideas he later wrote about "before he did" (278). She was interested in complex ethical issues such as whether intention is necessary for something to be considered a sin, a question he discussed in his *Ethics*. Abelard and Heloise were thinkers, not just lovers, but while he is remembered as both, she has become lover only, her powerful intellect forgotten.

In addition to scholarly works about theology, Abelard's letters to Heloise survive (not love letters, but solemn letters from abbot to abbess about how to govern her convent), as does his *Historia Calamitatum,* or *The History of My Misfortunes.* He ordered the work to be copied and disseminated so that all of Europe would know about his life, his work, and his distress. We learn not only of his studies but of his affair with Heloise. He tells us bluntly that when Fulbert gave him full control over Heloise, he used that freedom to his advantage, starting a passionate affair with her. "In short," Abelard writes, "our desires left no stage of love-making untried, and if love could devise something new, we welcomed it" (Radice 1974, 67–8). Heloise got pregnant and had a son (named Astrolabe!). Abelard and Heloise were secretly married, but Heloise was deeply unhappy because she believed marriage would ruin Abelard's career in the church. Abelard sent Heloise off to a convent, against her wishes. She stayed, however, eventually becoming the abbess. After the affair and the secret marriage, Heloise's Uncle Fulbert was furious: he and his servants sought Abelard out and, as Abelard puts it, "they cut off the parts of my body whereby I had committed the wrong of which they complained" (Radice 1974, 75).

Abelard and Heloise's affair has already begun at the beginning of *Spider's Voice.* Abelard hires Spider as a servant because he was born mute. He can reveal the affair with neither his voice nor in writing, because as a peasant, he cannot read or write. It is to Spider, according to the premise of the novel, that we owe the existence of Heloise's letters to Abelard. Like Evyn and Juliana of *The King's Shadow* and *The Striped Ships,* Spider contributes to the survival of what has become a famous document.

The second story in *Spider's Voice* belongs not to Abelard and Heloise, but to Spider himself, whose real name is Aran. Born to a family of shepherds, Aran is left alone in the world when his mother dies and he escapes his cruel father and brother. Because he is mute, they think he must be stupid, as well. But the Parisian dealer in human freaks and marvels who buys Aran from his brother knows he has his wits. Aran is welded into a metal tube to make his body remain small while his limbs grow long and spider-like. Later, he is to be sold into some high-ranking noble's home as an entertainment piece. This is the fate from which Abelard rescues Spider, storming in like the cavalry with his students, freeing Spider from the metal tube as well as from the freak-seller. Abelard takes Spider into his home as his servant and treats him as if he has a brain. No wonder Spider sees Abelard as a hero.

Skurzynski, on the other hand, does not think Peter Abelard is as splendid as Spider does. Although Spider tells us over and over again how much he admires Abelard, and although Abelard's students worship him, Skurzynski does not portray Abelard in a way that helps readers to love him. Indeed, it's difficult for anyone who has read the

Historia Calamitatum to find him charming. Consider his estimation of Heloise—and of himself:

> I considered all the usual attractions for a lover and decided she was the one to bring to my bed, confident that I should have an easy success; for at that time I had youth and exceptional good looks as well as my great reputation to recommend me, and feared no rebuff from any woman I might choose to honour with my love. (Radice 1974, 66)

Since Abelard frees Spider from a horrendous fate, however, we can readily understand his admiration for Abelard, especially when we consider that Abelard was a very popular, good-looking, and charismatic teacher whose university students, all young boys and men, flocked to him and joined in his causes. Although Skurzynski shows us the crowds of devoted students and tells us how much Spider admires him, Abelard's pride and pomposity also come through clearly in her portrayal of him. He does rescue Spider, but for his own purposes. The events and situations Skurzynski highlights from Abelard's life are often not very impressive. As the novel nears its conclusion, even Spider begins to realize Abelard's shortcomings, although like Heloise, he continues to love Abelard despite his faults.

Heloise is Skurzynski's real hero. She gives up everything for Abelard but Abelard is too self-absorbed to notice. It's Heloise who suggests that Abelard should teach Spider to read Latin, and later, she takes over his reading lessons herself. When Spider regains his voice, Heloise notices; Abelard does not. Heloise was enormously unusual in the twelfth century, being so well-educated, and Skurzynski's portrayal of her owes little to modern conceptions about gender roles and more to Heloise's own words in her letters to Abelard. Although Heloise's position may seem untenable to modern readers, it is too well documented to question: Heloise maintained her love for Abelard throughout her life. She defined this love partly as obedience to his wishes (although she often disagreed with him). She never wanted to marry Abelard because she did not want to sabotage either his fame or his possibility for advancement in the Church. Skurzynski includes Heloise's famous words on this subject in *Spider's Voice:* "I'd rather be mistress to *you* than wife to the king!" (89). Despite her strength, intelligence, and education, Heloise preferred to subordinate her own goals and desires to her lover's in ways modern readers might find unpalatable. Skurzynski, constrained by the surviving documents, makes Heloise a woman of her time.

Spider's Voice is historically accurate, with only a few lapses. Scholarship was the only way open to someone of Spider's class to change his status during the twelfth century. It was rare, but not completely unheard of, for a peasant to move away from a rural setting in this way. However, what is not realistic is the way Spider is taught. When Abelard begins to teach Spider to read Latin, he uses not a birch rod, but patience. When you consider that Abelard used violence (although he would never have considered it that) to instruct Heloise, it's hard to believe that he would abandon the tried and true methods when he began teaching Spider. Despite this inaccuracy, the texts Abelard chooses to teach Spider are appropriate to what we know of twelfth-century continental education: he begins with the "Our Father" (in Latin, of course) and moves on to his own difficult theological works, which he recites from memory (70). This point is particularly accurate. Clanchy says that a "really literate person, like Abelard or St. Bernard, did little reading and writing. Masters of the 'sacred page' [as the Bible and the works of the church fathers were called] knew the texts by heart and they composed by dictation" (1997, 63).

Spider is able to distance himself some from both Abelard and Heloise by the end of the novel. At the beginning of the story, he is a young, mute boy, abused by his family and his captor, entranced by Heloise's physical beauty and Abelard's charisma. By novel's end, he has matured enough to leave behind some of his idolization of the two; he begins to see them as complex people. Because he is able to travel to the separate religious houses where Abelard and Heloise live, he can speak with them, read their letters, and ruminate on their lives as well as on his own. Consider how different the story would be had it been told by one of the two lovers. By placing Spider in a position that allows him to speak with both and to bring them news of each other, we not only learn something of the difficulty of communication in an age that did not have the kind of technology we rely on, we also see both sides of the story.

Joan of Arc in *Young Joan* and *Dove and Sword*

Like the biographies of Heloise and Abelard, the life of the peasant girl who crowned the king of France before she was burned at the stake at nineteen is very well-documented. We have Joan's own words, the words she spoke at her trial of condemnation, which give us a sense of her as a person. We know about the saints and angels who appeared to her, telling her to take up arms: the Archangel Michael, Saints Catherine and Margaret. Her life in the village of Domrémy, her childhood friends and family, her spinning and plowing and watching of sheep in the pastures: all this we know from the transcripts of her trials. From the reports of her neighbors and friends, who testified during her trial of rehabilitation twenty-five years later, we know how pious and how good Joan was considered to be.

Joan lived in the late Middle Ages, during the Hundred Years' War, and died on May 30, 1431. Although she was a peasant, her father was a farmer who held considerable authority in the village of Domrémy. We learn much not only about Joan's life, but also of fifteenth-century habits, from her trial testimony. For example, when she is asked her age, Joan replies, "As far as I know, about nineteen years old" (Pernoud 1994, 15), a statement that reminds readers how differently the passage of time was treated in the Middle Ages. Our focus on exact ages and dates was foreign to most medieval people, who tended to count the passage of time in relation to important events, and to divide years into agricultural and liturgical seasons, not months. It was hardly unusual for someone not to know her exact age. In fact, as Regine Pernoud notes, "for the historian of the Middle Ages, the surprising thing would have been if Joan had known her age" (1994, 27). And consider how one of the king's esquires, a middle-aged man who presumably would have been well-educated, reports a date, linking an event to a Catholic feast day, not a day of a month: "Joan the Maid came to Vaucouleurs at the time of the Ascension of Our Lord" (Pernoud 1994, 33). (The Ascension takes place forty days after Easter.) His way of measuring time is reminiscent of that of the twelfth-century monk who wrote in *The Peterborough Chronicle* that something happened "on the Sunday when *Exsurge quare obdormis Domine* is sung [at Mass]" (Whitelock 1961, 194), a reference his monastic brethren would understand as easily as Joan of Arc and her family would recognize the "time of the Ascension of Our Lord."

From Joan's testimony, we also learn about medieval girls' education in rural communities. She says, "It was from my mother that I learnt Pater Noster, Ave Maria, Credo. Nobody taught me my belief, if not my mother" (Pernoud 1994, 15–16). Like most girls throughout the Middle Ages, Joan's mother was responsible for her formal education—her prayers—as well as her more informal education: sewing, spinning, keeping house. As her friends and neighbors report, Joan also helped cultivate the fields and watched the cattle and sheep, frequently spinning as she did the latter (16). They remember her piety, her willingness to go to confession, her giving of alms to the poor, and her hard work both inside and outside the house. One woman notes that Joan would give up her own bed to the poor (18).

Their testimony, and Joan's, also makes clear the tension that existed in the various regions of France during this time period. With English forces occupying much of France and no clear claimant to the French throne, loyalties were divided and villagers sometimes had to escape—with their animals—to another town or to a nearby fortified place in order to be protected from roving bands of soldiers. Because the neighboring village of Maxey was loyal to the Burgundians, while Domrémy villagers supported the dauphin (the title of the French crown prince), inhabitants of the two villages sometimes skirmished (20).

But amidst the tension, there was time for such celebration as the annual dance at the Ladies' Tree or the Fairies' Tree, a large beech tree near Joan's village that was reputed to be a place where fairies danced. One villager said that "in times past" a knight met his lady, who was a fairy, under the tree—a story she says she has "heard read out of a romance" (Pernoud 1994, 23). (Notice that she did not read the story herself but heard someone else reading it aloud.) Another villager reports that no one she knew ever saw fairies actually dancing there (22). Near the tree was a spring whose waters were supposed to having curative powers, although Joan herself expresses some doubt about whether the water could actually cure people. To celebrate the arrival of spring, the young people of Domrémy danced under the tree and hung it with garlands in honor of the Virgin Mary, thus wedding folk practices with Catholicism. No one saw any discrepancy between Catholicism and the ancient Celtic traditions of the Ladies' Tree. Keep in mind that the villagers who reported these things were speaking to Church inquisitors and that Joan's heterodoxy was the question being examined—had this information seemed heretical to them, they would hardly have been so free with it. Michael Clanchy reminds us that the borders between science, magic, and religion, all of which dealt "with invisible forces at work in the world," are hard to define when we consider the Middle Ages (1997, 26).

As they danced under the tree, village boys and girls ate special cakes their mothers baked for them. Sometimes the lords and ladies of Domrémy, not just the peasants, ate under the tree, as well, although at a physical distance from each other that reflected their social distance.

When she was thirteen, Joan first heard the voices of the three saints who spoke with her, guiding her in her quest to see the French king crowned. She found a way to get herself introduced to Robert de Baudricourt, an army captain loyal to the dauphin, and convinced him of the sincerity of her visions and her quest. With his help, Joan was presented to the dauphin, and in a famous episode, she immediately recognized him even though he disguised himself. She was able to convince him "of her divine mission to help drive the English from France and to assist at his overdue coronation" (Solon 1982, 114). After the church authorities examined her claims to divine guidance for legitimacy, Joan was given a leading position in the army, which won important battles, such as the one that freed the city of Orléans, which had been besieged by the English. From 1429–1430, Joan led armies and won battles that led to the dauphin being crowned King Charles VII of France. But when she was captured in battle, the king did not ransom her, since her political usefulness had passed. Instead, he allowed the English to imprison, try, and finally burn her at the stake for heresy. Almost a quarter of a century later, an inquiry into her original trial—during which time her friends and neighbors were interviewed by an inquisitor, an official representative of the Pope—found the trial to have been invalid and Joan's good name was restored. However, it wasn't until the nineteenth century that she became "a popular national heroine," and not until 1920 did she become a saint (Solon 1982, 115).

Many impressively-researched biographies of Joan exist, and she stars in several novels for adults and young adults. The two I will focus on here tell her story from very different places and perspectives: *Young Joan* by Barbara Dana, ends before Joan takes up the sword. In *Dove and Sword: A Novel of Joan of Arc*, Nancy Garden's Joan is already wearing armor and fighting for the dauphin. While Dana's Joan narrates her own story from the first-person viewpoint, Garden chooses Gabrielle, an invented character, to tell the tale. Both novels, however, cleave closely to the documents about Joan's life, and many of the same villagers, soldiers, settings, and events come to life in the two works. Joan's brothers, Pierre and Jean, her mother and father, her friends Hauviette and Mengette, Henri, a boy from her village, and others who testified in her trial, appear in both novels, although they take on different roles and their importance in Joan's life varies.

Dana's novel is written for a younger audience than Garden's. Her Joan stays close to the Joan of the trial transcripts, with the attitudes of a fifteenth-century peasant, not a modern teenager. The trial for the reader is that Young Joan is so very, very good that readers might wish she could be a little bit horrid. But not Joan. She feels joy in her heart at moments when the rest of us would be filled with annoyance, when we would weep and whine and moan. Dana's Joan never minds the hard work required of a fifteenth-century peasant. When she helps her mother spin wool all day long, her arms ache, but she says, "my heart would be joyful, my mind always willing to keep with the work" (91). The danger in having Joan—whom we know to have been exceedingly good—narrate her own story, is in turning readers off by her excessive sweetness and her propensity to find joy in even the most burdensome of daily tasks. Were Joan to be dropped into her readers' world, her heart would be filled with bliss were she told to clean the bathroom, rake the leaves, or take out the trash. All that goodness can be a little tiresome. Because her fellow villagers are as sweet and kind as Joan (although they don't pray as much), her goodness doesn't set her apart from them, and the book seems more a Sunday-school lesson than a piece of historical fiction.

Garden's French villagers have more spice and a little less sugar. In the beginning of *Dove and Sword,* Joan (called Jeannette and later, Jeanne) is already a distant character. She is older than Gabrielle, the narrator, who shares a close friendship with Joan's brother Pierre. Gabrielle and Pierre spy on Joan when she talks with her saints, and she seems frighteningly strange to them. They wonder whether she is holy or possessed. Gabrielle's older sister Catherine makes fun of Joan, who seems a little too good and holy to Catherine and some of the other villagers. In fact, when Gabrielle and Pierre tell a little girl that she will win a prize if she is as good as Joan, the child gives up imme- diately, knowing she can't be *that* good (19). These opinions echo those of Joan's friend Mengette, who at Joan's trial of reconciliation said that Joan was "so good, simple and pious that I and the other young girls would tell her that she was too pious" (Pernoud 1994, 17). In Garden's novel, Gabrielle wonders some about Joan's goodness: If she prays when she should be watching the sheep or spinning, does that make her less good? Good in a different way? By allowing a different charac- ter to narrate the story, Garden avoids the problem inherent in Joan's goodness.

From her narrative stance, it is clear that Dana, who as an actress has played the role of Joan of Arc, feels very positively towards her character. Garden's stance is more complex: she seems to both admire Joan and to find her as unearthly as the people of Domrémy found her. Early on, Gabrielle tells us that she "had always thought Jeannette rather dull" (12), although later she comes to admire Joan, and the reader may suspect that we are hearing the author's own opinion. In other places, we do hear the author speaking through Gabrielle, espe- cially in her disapproval of war as a way to solve problems. Because Gabrielle works as a healer, traveling with Joan's army, she sees and experiences the wounds and scars, including the emotional scars caused by loss of loved ones, that war visits upon people. Sometimes, in Gabrielle's view, Joan seems to be motivated by anger and a desire for vengeance, not by God, and she sends men and boys into battle because of this motivation. The novel almost turns into a polemic at the end, when Garden, through Gabrielle, inveighs against war. Both Garden and Gabrielle find Joan too much the hawk, and the novel ends with a long anti-war paragraph in which Gabrielle tries to reconcile her admi- ration for Joan with her dislike of Joan's methods. Gabrielle's words, which end the novel, sound much like Garden's: "Maybe someday, far in the future, someone will find a way, and thus end war. But how will there be a future if a way is not found, and if wars continue?" (236). Character and author meld together, and medieval and modern view- points coalesce.

Both *Young Joan* and *Dove and Sword* capture the feel of life in fifteenth-century Europe, with the constant threat of attack by brigands and the constant labor of peasant life. In portraying fifteenth-century language patterns, however, they differ. Dana falls prey to what Miriam Youngerman Miller calls "strangling archaism" (1995, 88) when she tries to convey medieval-sounding dialogue. She inverts word-order, particularly the word *not,* with the result that Joan's speech and even her thoughts sound stilted and strange: "You remember it not?" "He liked that not" (43), Joan says, and she thinks, in this convoluted passage, "I had not the knowing until just before that I would be allowed to join in the work" (158). You mean you didn't know if they'd let you help? the reader wants to ask. Miller's discussion of the way writers for young adults convey language in novels with medieval settings indicates that there are more creative ways to use language in order to evoke medieval linguistic patterns. Garden's language does not call attention to itself in the way Dana's does, although she includes a few sentences with inverted word order and archaic diction: "'Tis you, Brother Antoine; how you did affright me!'" we hear one character say, for example (55), and another asks, "How came you here?" (40). Very few sentences of this ilk are to be found in the novel, however. To remind readers that the tale is set in France, Garden sprinkles her text with occasional French words, always followed by an English translation: "'Merci, merci,' she said. 'Thank you, thank you!'" (29). Because Garden only occasionally uses unusual word order or French words, and never in an intrusive way, they do not take away from the narrative in the way Dana's convoluted word order does.

Issues of gender, class, and literacy, on the other hand, do occasionally intrude in *Dove and Sword,* when Gabrielle becomes Garden's mouthpiece. As I have already noted in Chapter One, Gabrielle values reading as an avenue to medical knowledge to an unrealistic degree. Her views on gender and class are equally modern ones, and Garden becomes a little heavy-handed when she tries to teach her readers that war is bad, reading is good, all people are created equal, and girls can do whatever they want to do. Maybe in modern America, but not in fifteenth-century France. When Gabrielle meets Christine de Pisan, a historical figure famous for earning her living by writing, Garden is at her most didactic, with thinly-veiled lessons about women's contributions to medicine. Christine wrote a poem in praise of Joan of Arc, and this fact provides a connection between the high-born Christine and Gabrielle the peasant. Christine teaches Gabrielle to read in both French and Latin so she can become a better healer by reading the books of Dame Trotula and Hildegard of Bingen, both real women of the medieval period. In one long paragraph, Christine catalogues all the women physicians there have been (185), and it's hard for the readers not to feel we're being taught a lesson.

We know early on that Gabrielle wants to become a healer instead of marrying and having children, even though her model of a healer is her mother, who married, had children, and continued to practice healing. Although Gabrielle is close to her mother and learns herblore and midwifery from her, she takes comfort and courage from Joan's refusal to marry. Gabrielle is saddened when her family rejoices at the birth of a son, but not a daughter. "That seemed wrong, for without women to bear sons, and nurture them, and heal them, there would be no sons at all. So was not the one worth at least as much as the other?" (27). It does seem wrong, and one is worth as much as the other—for a modern audience, but not necessarily for a medieval one, particularly since in much of the medieval period, a son was necessary in order to inherit land and keep it in the family. The reader may wonder whose voice we are hearing here: Gabrielle's or Garden's?

Later, Gabrielle falls in love and decides both to marry and to study medicine. Here, modern attitudes towards class, not just education and literacy, creep into the novel. The boy Gabrielle loves is Louis, the son of a nobleman, who returns her affections. While it's true that war can both raise and lower fortunes, Louis's easy ability to overcome class distinctions seems a little difficult to accept. Neither he nor Gabrielle sees any problems in their relationship, and they plan to marry. Two neutral voices, Joan of Arc's mother, Isabelle, and Henri, a boy from Gabrielle's village, sound warnings about the impracticality of such a marriage. Garden does recognize the difficulties of a relationship between people of very different social statuses in the fifteenth century: She avoids these difficulties by killing off Louis and sending Gabrielle to a convent to live out her life as a healer. With this neat solution Garden indulges her readers' taste for a Cinderella-style romance at the same time as she remains true to the marital practices of the period.

Garden's attitude towards class, which she anachronistically imposes on her medieval characters, becomes apparent when the king grants Joan's family the patent of nobility. Garden gives some of the players in *Dove and Sword* attitudes that seem more fitting for a contemporary mind than a medieval one: They embrace the American ideal that all people are created equal and class does not matter. In the novel, characters the reader values do not value class distinctions. Joan's good brother Pierre is scornful of his new nobility, whereas Jean, the profligate brother, flaunts his new status. Jean is more believable than Pierre. It is likely that a medieval peasant who had just become a member of the nobility would be as thrilled as a modern American who just won the lottery.

It's difficult for a modern writer to tell a tale set in a time period that has different values than our own yet still create role models with attitudes the writer believes are appropriate. One way to avoid this issue is to use time travel as a device. A modern teen can comment on medieval practices without creating anachronisms. Marie D. Goodwin looks at differences between medieval and modern attitudes towards gender and religion in *Where the Towers Pierce the Sky* (1989), a novel in which Joan of Arc is a peripheral character. An alchemist's mistake results in Lizzie, a thoroughly modern teenager, being sent to the fifteenth century. Lizzie is shocked when Jacques, a medieval French boy, wonders why she is not married at the age of thirteen; Jacques is even more shocked to learn that Lizzie is not a Catholic. He "stared at her as if she'd confessed to boiling babies for breakfast" (24). Then it's Lizzie's turn to be appalled at Jacques' attitude towards Jews. "Simon's not a Christ-killer!" Lizzie says. "He wasn't *around* when Christ died, idiot!" (100). Goodwin never allows these issues to be resolved: Lizzie never convinces Jacques to think the way she does. Medieval and modern attitudes remain different.

Dropping a modern character into a medieval setting as Goodwin does gives writers a device to explore differences since the character gets to ask the questions and think the thoughts of the reader. Revealing those differences entirely from the point of view of medieval characters is much more challenging. The author must find ways to present differences without commenting directly on them. Just as we would find little noteworthy about highways and the smell of french-fries wafting out of fast-food establishments, a medieval teenager would find unpaved streets and the smell of rotting vegetables or raw sewage as unremarkable as attitudes towards religion, class, gender, and literacy. Some of these attitudes are problematic in Scott O'Dell's *The Road to Damietta*. O'Dell is less successful than Skurzynski, Garden, and Dana in creating an authentically medieval character. His protagonist has more in common with Goodwin's Lizzie than with Spider or Gabrielle, who despite a few inaccuracies, remain medieval teenagers.

St. Francis of Assisi and *The Road to Damietta*

Like Gabrielle of *Dove and Sword* and Spider in *Spider's Voice*, an invented character reveals incidents from the life of a historical person in Scott O'Dell's *The Road to Damietta*. In the early thirteenth century, Ricca di Montanaro, a wealthy young Italian girl, is in love with the man who will become St. Francis of Assisi. Readers see Francis's conversion from the wealthy son of a cloth merchant, concerned with material goods, the trappings of chivalry, and having fun, to a religious man who takes the words of the Gospel literally: Francis gave up everything he had to live by begging and to serve the poor. The novel includes the famous scene in which Francis strips off his clothes in front of the church, literally and metaphorically rejecting his father's trade and wealth. Afterwards, Francis lived in caves and abandoned churches, which he rebuilt. Like Abelard, Francis was a charismatic leader, and followers soon joined him. In the year 1209, Francis was received by the Pope, who officially recognized this new way of life, which became known as the Franciscan Order, or the Friars Minor. The friars followed Jesus's admonitions to preach, to live in poverty, and to heal the sick, found in Matthew 10. The Poor Clares, an organization for women who wanted to follow Francis's way of life, began in 1212, when a wealthy, noble girl from Assisi joined Francis. A few years later, Francis tried to convert the Muslims to Christianity and he preached before a sultan in Egypt. During his lifetime, rifts opened up in the Franciscan Order, especially regarding ownership of property (Little 1982, 191–2). By the fourteenth century, friars had not only split into four subgroups (Franciscans, Dominicans, Carmelites, and Augustinians), they had also gained a bad reputation, so bad that some people associated them with the anti-Christ. Think of Chaucer's Friar, from the *General Prologue* to *The Canterbury Tales*—he corrupts most of the ideals Francis lived by. Chaucer's Friar loves good food, good wine, and pretty women, and he can't be bothered to help the poor, who seem like a nuisance to him. Although there were plenty of good men who became friars, the ones who got the press were corrupt, often horrifyingly so.

In *The Road to Damietta*, however, friars are still brand new, and Francis is beloved of many, both before and after his conversion. In the novel's beginning, he is a popular, fashionable, sensitive young fop who is deeply offended by the smell of a leper and who takes part in the semi-pagan town revels. By the novel's end, however, he has become a pious Christian who lives quite literally according to the Gospel, ministering especially to lepers. The story of his conversion runs parallel to the tale of Ricca di Montanaro and her unfulfilled love for Francis.

Like *Spider's Voice* and *Dove and Sword,* this novel reveals the biography of the famous person obliquely, through the voice of an invented character. However, we see far less of Francis than we did of Abelard and Heloise or Joan of Arc; the focus remains squarely on Ricca di Montanaro. Ricca is even more well-educated and urbane than Heloise. In *Spider's Voice,* Skurzynski makes it clear that Heloise's education was unusual. O'Dell, on the other hand, does not indicate that Ricca's learning might be extraordinary. The daughter of a wealthy Italian merchant of the early thirteenth century, she reads and writes in Italian, Latin, even Arabic, and her tutor familiarizes her with Muslim and Buddhist parables. Thirteen years old at the novel's start, Ricca develops a crush on Francis Bernadone, the wealthy young man who is admired by most of the women in Assisi. Like Saint Augustine, whose *Confessions* Ricca copies, Francis is a profligate youth who leaves behind his wildness when he embraces Christianity. Ricca never gives up hope that Francis will convert back to his old ways and grow to love her. Her tutor, Raul, gives her the letters of Heloise to read as an admonition against her love for Francis. Ricca, however, sends Francis letters in which she copies passages about the famous love affair and pretends to have questions about Abelard and Heloise. Francis remains distant throughout the novel. He speaks kindly to Ricca, but never in great depth, as she continues her embarrassing pursuit of him. O'Dell takes no stand on the saint, portraying him in neutral terms.

The novel veers between being very historically accurate and not at all so. The portrayal of Francis, which follows official accounts, is consistent with our knowledge of medieval life. It's with Ricca, the invented character, the one whose mind the reader enters, that the inaccuracies become apparent. Ricca's level of education, particularly her fluency in Arabic, is questionable. Also problematic is the presentation of books and writing. For example, Ricca spends a lot of time copying texts and she chooses which script to write in as her fancy pleases her. At one point, she decides to change her regular Gothic writing for a Carolingian alphabet, because she finds the latter more feminine (94). Since Carolingian scripts were used during the time of Charlemagne, who was crowned Emperor of the Holy Roman Empire in the year 800, and since Ricca lives around the year 1220, this would be like a modern teen deciding to use the Elizabethan script that Shakespeare wrote in. Professional scribes spent years learning the intricacies of particular scripts, and for Ricca to pick and choose between them as if she were selecting fonts on a computer devalues scribal training and skill. All that medieval handwriting may simply look archaic to general readers, but historians who study the Middle Ages are often able to date manuscripts by their scripts, and Carolingian scripts belong to the Carolingian period just as surely as Gothic scripts belong to the Gothic period.

In matters of class, Ricca is a girl of her own century; in terms of gender and religion, however, she sometimes speaks for the author, professing opinions too modern to be believable. As a member of the di Montanaro family, Ricca has many servants, most of whom have neither names nor personalities. To Ricca, they exist to serve and she feels no emotion or loyalty towards them. When she passes a leper, cast out of Assisi by the law Ricca's father helped to write, she is offended by the sight. Although Ricca gives a flower to a leper at the end of the novel, in homage to the memory of Francis who took lepers as his special charge, the vast gulf between the leper's status and her own is evident in her actions. She bestows the flower in an act of noblesse oblige, not of solidarity. In these ways, Ricca's attitudes towards those of different social status befit a girl of her time period.

When it comes to gender roles and comparative religion, however, Ricca sometimes seems more like a modern than a medieval teenager. During a long stay in a convent, where her father sends her as a punishment for her forward ways, Ricca copies Augustine's *Confessions*. Coming to the parts about Augustine's treatment of women and his views towards them, Ricca changes the words around, making them more palatable to herself—and to modern readers. "For instance," she says, "early in the *Confessions*, where the saint wrote that he 'should not believe many things concerning himself on the authority of feeble women,' I removed the word 'feeble.' I also straightened out several other things that I found belittling." She finds the work irritating and tires "of the endless talk about salvation" (145). Augustine is one of the four Fathers of the Church, revered throughout the medieval period, and Ricca's words about him—and particularly her changing of his words—is tantamount to blasphemy.

Compare Ricca's act here with that of a historical figure, Eadmer. Eadmer was a twelfth-century English monk who wrote a biography of Anselm, Archbishop of Canterbury (who died in 1109). Eadmer's biography was extraordinary in many ways. First of all, it treated Anselm like a person, not a formulaic saint, as earlier biographies of religious figures had done. Eadmer included speech and details of daily life, details he scribbled on wax tablets throughout the time Anselm lived at Canterbury. But most importantly, Eadmer was as disobedient as Ricca to church authority. When Anselm decided that a biography glorified the person too much at the expense of God he, Eadmer's superior, ordered Eadmer to destroy the work. As you read Eadmer's version of this episode, keep in mind that a monk takes a vow of obedience to his monastic superiors. "Moreover," Eadmer writes, "when I had first taken the work in hand, and had already transcribed onto parchment a great part of what I had drafted in wax, Father Anselm himself one day called me to him privately and asked what it was I was drafting and copying" (Southern 1972, 150). Eadmer showed Anselm the biography, and Anselm read and corrected it. However, a few days later, according to Eadmer, "the archbishop called me to him, and ordered me to destroy entirely the quires in which I had put together the work. . . . This was certainly a severe blow to me. Nevertheless, I dared not entirely disobey his command, and yet I was not willing to lose altogether a work which I had put together with much labour. So I observed the letter of his command, and destroyed those quires, having first copied their contents onto other quires" (Southern 1972, 150–51). Like Ricca, Eadmer has a strong sense of his own individuality, and confidence in his own opinion, confidence enough to allow him to commit sins. Unlike Ricca, however, he recognizes his sins for what they are and asks readers to pray for him. He is disobedient because he believes Anselm's greatness—not his own—should be recorded for posterity. Ricca's act of revising Augustine, on the other hand, suggests that she believes her own ideas are as worth recording as the saint's. She worries not a whit about the salvation of her soul.

Changing the words to suit her own opinions is a tool Ricca uses later, as well, when she serves as Francis's translator. First, however, she tries to persuade Francis, who plans to travel to Egypt during the Fifth Crusade in order to convert the sultan to Christianity, to abandon his quest. Ricca tells Francis, "Being a Moslem, the sultan will never listen to you" (160). Her views on the crusades and on the sultan's religion are very different from those of Francis, of Bishop Pelagius, who leads the Crusade, in fact, of everyone she comes into contact with. She understands, in ways the others—even Francis—do not, the horror of the Crusades. Her own presence in Egypt, whence she travels aboard a ship of kindhearted prostitutes in an episode that strains credulity, has nothing to do with religion and everything to do with her love for Francis, whom she follows. As a fluent speaker of Arabic, Ricca acts as a translator when Francis meets the sultan and she tempers the words Francis speaks so that the sultan will not be offended. The sultan is amused by Francis and by Ricca's unrequited love for him, and offers peace, which the crusaders do not accept. In this section of the novel, Ricca seems very modern, especially since her attitudes differ so much from those around her. O'Dell portrays thirteenth-century adults, including highly-educated churchmen, as unsophisticated fools in comparison to the adolescent Ricca, who is the only character who understands the world from a modern perspective. This lack of sophistication on the part of the adults is further underscored when we remember that throughout the novel, Ricca is portrayed as childish and self-centered.

However, O'Dell's portrait of popular Christianity is more historically accurate. Ricca's mother is characterized by her faith: she often sees visions and demons. Ricca and the rest of her family neither accept nor reject these manifestations of the unknown, but they agree with them in order to keep the peace. Ricca reports her mother's visions very matter-of-factly: During an exorcism, her mother sees three demons, "two oldsters and a mean young one—leap through the window. To their deaths, she was sure" (41). "She frequently saw these apparitions," Ricca says, "and usually, to be a comfort, I saw them too" (43). Although Ricca does not see the visions, neither does she deny their existence.

Ricca's attitudes and reactions reveal her to be a modern teenager trapped in a medieval culture. Like Elenor in Frances Temple's *The Ramsay Scallop*, Ricca seems too wise for her age and status. Yet readers can still find value in *The Road to Damietta*. Some will be introduced to Francis of Assisi, others will be surprised to find that urban centers, not just rural, agricultural areas, played a role in the European Middle Ages. And readers can react to the text, examining it critically, asking which actions of Ricca's are appropriate for a medieval adolescent and which are not. Flawed portraits of historical periods can be valuable if they are read with a critical eye. However, the most inventive writers find ways of smoothly illustrating differences between modern and medieval culture, be they matters of class and gender, of literacy and education, of attitudes towards authority or religion, without creating characters with anachronistic attitudes.

Chapter Six

Of Commoners and Kings
Medievalism in Fantasy Novels

In a college Adolescent Literature class, a student told me she didn't like Karen Cushman's *The Midwife's Apprentice* (1995) because it wasn't about a princess. When she saw it was set "back then," she assumed the novel would have magic in it, too. But it didn't: another disappointment. Then a graduate student, preparing to lead a group of junior high school students in a discussion of Robin McKinley's fantasy novel *The Hero and the Crown* (1984), asked me about the way the medieval period was presented in the book. Where do students get this idea that fantasy and the Middle Ages are interchangeable, and that the Middle Ages consisted of princesses, kings, magic, and fancy swordplay? Among other places, from their teachers. In their book, *From Hinton to Hamlet: Building Bridges Between Young Adult Literature and the Classics* (1996), Susan Herz and Donald Gallo point their readers towards several novels related to the Middle Ages. In addition to Cushman's *Catherine, Called Birdy* (1994) and *The Midwife's Apprentice* and *Adam of the Road* (1942) by Elizabeth Janet Gray, Herz and Gallo suggest *The Hero and the Crown* and Tamora Pierce's fantasy series, *The Lioness Quartet* (86). Only three out of five of these titles are historical novels set in the Middle Ages.

Only three out of five? Perhaps you think I should be realistic, cheering Herz and Gallo for getting it more than half right. And given the confusion about the medieval period, maybe I should.

Many of the ideas that we find in modern fantasy novels have their origins in medieval beliefs as well as in medieval fantasy literature. Perhaps this confusion about the place of magic and monsters adds to the confusion between historical and fantasy fiction. Some novels, like *The Hobbit* (1937), we can easily and definitely label fantasy. Others, like

79

Dove and Sword: A Novel of Joan of Arc (1995), can just as easily be categorized as historical fiction. Between the two is a range of novels that combine elements of both genres.

Look at Cynthia Voigt's enchanting novel, *Jackaroo* (1985). It's sometimes labeled historical fiction, as, for example in Karen Smith's *School Library Journal* review (1985, 96). Why? It's set in a non-industrial, agricultural society and the speech patterns include some archaic-sounding phrases like "Think you?" and "Osh, aye." There are illiterate peasants and lords and ladies and even, somewhere in the distance, a king. Some people ride horses, others carry swords. How much more medieval can you get?

Plenty.

For example, you can set a novel in a recognizable time and place, say Paris in 1117, instead of an invented kingdom. Or you can people it with historical characters, like King Charles VII of France, instead of an invented Earl Sutherland. *The Ramsay Scallop* (1994) contains no easily-recognizable historical characters, but it's set in England and Europe, one character has just returned from the Crusades, and all the characters travel on a pilgrimage to an actual place. *The Midwife's Apprentice* takes place in an invented village, but we know the village is in England and a brief mention of King Edward, known as Longshanks, places the novel between the years 1272 and 1307. Looked at in these ways, *Jackaroo* hardly fits a definition of historical fiction.

But is it a fantasy novel? Writing in the *Wilson Library Journal*, Patty Campbell says *Jackaroo* is "a fine strong fantasy" (1986, 50). Yet there are no elves, just stories about them. There are no dragons, no monsters, no magic, none of the usual trappings of fantasy literature. Instead, we have a realistic story set in a carefully-conceived and utterly convincing kingdom inhabited by complex, believable characters. Perhaps it's the medieval-sounding setting that causes readers to label it a fantasy. Look at the ways history and fantasy get blurred by some critics: In an article about *Jackaroo* Jim Garrison tells us the novel is "set somewhere in the Middle Ages" (1996, 12) while Suzanne Reid, in *Presenting Cynthia Voigt* (1995), calls it a historical romance "set in a medieval feudal era" (62). However, on the next page, Reid first calls Voigt's "history" "imagined" and then tells us the novel "occurs in a northern European land" (63). Is this history? Fantasy? What are readers to think?

Cathi Dunn MacRae provides a helpful description when she says that Voigt "imports realism into an otherworld without magic" (1998, 149). Also helpful is the review in *The Bulletin of the Center for Children's Books* which tells us that *Jackaroo* has a "romantic/medieval milieu" (1985, 19). Among other aspects that contribute to the novel's medieval milieu are the representations of literacy, gender, and class and the portrayal of a homogeneous, rigidly hierarchical society, the King-dom. Although the setting is not historical, Voigt draws on history for many of her details, from the swords the soldiers carry to the quill pen the steward writes with to the grain and turnips eaten by the poor. The portrayal of women's hard lot in life and the dowry a woman's family must pay to see her married, the details of an inn's daily work—straw mattresses, bags of flour, ale to be brewed and horses to be curried—all could be taken from a textbook about medieval peasant life. Food consists of goat's milk and cheese, ale and apple pastry, and stews made of turnips, onions, and meat. (Voigt also includes potatoes as a foodsource in the Kingdom. Although potatoes sound authentically medieval, Spanish explorers didn't introduce them to Europe until the Renaissance.)

People in *Jackaroo* have a close relationship with nature, largely based on agriculture and their need for food and warmth, just as the medieval European peasantry did. The rigid stratification of classes also rings true: nobles with recognizable titles like king, earl, and lord treat peasants like chattels and Gwyn, the book's peasant heroine, never even entertains fantasies about serving the nobility, let alone marrying into it, the idea is so unrealistic to her. Equally unrealistic to Gwyn, but a comfort to many others of her social class, are the old tales of elves and dwarves and other marvels, tales that would have comforted or frightened medieval audiences as well. C.W. Sullivan's discussion of the fantasy novelist's use of traditional folk material is pertinent here. Such material, particularly as Voigt so skillfully employs it, provides what Neil Grobman has called "verisimilitude and local color" to the in-vented society, making it seem real because its traditional practices are similar to ones "the reader knows" (Sullivan 1992, 145). The reader knows legends about Robin Hood, for example, so the Kingdom's own legend of a Robin Hood figure named Jackaroo, who has a variety of tales attached to him, rings true. J.R.R. Tolkien uses a similar strategy in his Middle Earth books, incorporating both familiar and invented proverbs, as Sullivan has shown: "Bilbo's 'Escaping goblins to be caught by wolves' became, Tolkien tells us, 'a proverb, though we now say "out of the frying-pan into the fire" in the same sort of uncomfortable situ-ation'" (1992, 146). The weaving of familiar folk elements into an in-vented world can provide such verisimilitude that readers might easily have trouble distinguishing between fantasy and history.

What's missing, then, besides a recognizable place and time, that makes *Jackaroo* unhistorical? Were it set in medieval Europe, Christian-ity would necessarily be a part of the hierarchy, yet there is little men-tion of any religion. Gwyn's father buys Burl from the priests, whom we never see, and at deaths, no priest gives last rites. Once a year, we are told, a priest travels to each village to say prayers for all who have died that year. Moreover, bodies are burned, not buried, as they are in the medieval Christian church. But even more important, when Gwyn recites a rhyme that defines the circular social order of the kingdom, she doesn't mention God: "The land serves the people, the people serve the Lords, the Lords serve the Earls, the Earls serve the King, and the King serves the land" (251). To make this social order authentically medieval God would be above all, the angels below God, and finally, humans.

No Christianity, then. What else? In *Jackaroo,* only the lords are allowed to read. Were the novel set in medieval Europe, literacy would not be forbidden to the peasantry, as it was to slaves during the period when Americans practiced slavery. It's as dangerous for Gaderian, a lord's son, to teach Gwyn to read as it is for an escaped slave to teach the young slave girl Sarny in Gary Paulsen's novel, *Nightjohn* (1993). Like Sarny, but unlike a historical medieval peasant, Gwyn must keep her new-found knowledge carefully hidden. However, the presentation of Gwyn's journey to literacy is particularly convincing. She learns her letters not from a deep desire to better herself, but out of sheer boredom, when she and Gaderian are trapped by snow for twelve long days. And Gwyn's literacy remains rudimentary: when she needs to contact Gaderian later, she scratches an initial onto a piece of wax instead of writing a complete sentence. Consistent with her character, practical-minded Gwyn uses literacy as a tool. For her, it's little different than a saddle or a basket—simply a device that helps her accomplish a necessary task. She doesn't revere writing the way some of the characters discussed in Chapter One do, and in this way, Gwyn seems more like a medieval girl than some of the characters from historical novels. So, although *Jackaroo* is not historical fiction, its setting is convincing and would not be a bad way for readers to see some aspects of medieval culture.

The setting and inhabitants of *The Hero and the Crown* are equally convincing, but pure fantasy. Wherein lies the difference? Like *Jackaroo*, the setting is non-industrial and non-technological. Humans have a close relationship with nature. Fighters use swords, writers, quill pens. So far, so medieval. But Aerin's world is inhabited by humans as well as by the hafor, a dwarf-like race of people, by dragons and demons and sorcerers with magical powers. Aerin drinks malak with her turpi, and surka trees (whose leaves only royalty can touch) grow in the castle courtyard. Aerin's father may be the king, but the title for nobility is *sol*, not lord or earl. All of these are McKinley's inventions. Aerin spends her time fighting dragons; she visits places where time is elusive, where years pass but she doesn't age. This is the realm of fantasy, not history.

The fabulous creatures that populate Aerin's world can also be found in the imaginations and the old stories of the Kingdom's humans inhabitants in *Jackaroo*. Both high- and low-born people tell each other stories of dragons and elves, just as many medieval people did. Fantasy literature was as popular in the Middle Ages as it is now. Just as modern readers love the dragon fights in *The Hero and the Crown*, or the dwarves and elves and hobbits and dragons of Middle Earth, so did medieval readers enjoy tales of monsters and dragons in *Beowulf* and *The Nibelungenlied*. Look to the poems of the twelfth-century writer Marie de France and you will find a handsome knight transforming himself into a bird in order to visit the woman he loves, who is imprisoned in a tall tower. Or a man cursed to live three days of each week as a werewolf. Merlin the magician is a medieval creation, as is King Arthur's enchanted sword: as long as he wears the scabbard, he can't be killed. Chaucer's squire tells a story that includes a magic ring that allows its wearer to understand the birds and a magic horse made of brass that will bear its rider anywhere in the world within the space of twenty-four hours. A magician shows people visions in *The Franklin's Tale*, and fairies dance in a ring in *The Wife of Bath's Tale*. Middle English writers reveled in monsters and giants and heroes to fight them. In *Mimesis*, Erich Auerbach says these medieval tales were "an escape into fable and fairy tale" (1957, 120), which is how they function for modern readers as well. Marie and Chaucer and other medieval writers don't expect their audiences to think they are reporting facts any more than Robin McKinley does.

Nevertheless, there was a belief in the supernatural and its creatures during the Middle Ages. In *The Anglo-Saxon Chronicle*, dragons are reported to have been seen flying through the air, portending disaster. Some Anglo-Saxon charms fuse Christian and older beliefs in an effort to ward off elves or elf-shot. Particularly in the later Middle Ages, witches and heretics were closely linked. Both were sought out to be punished or destroyed by the Catholic Church. Joan of Arc was suspected of sorcery and therefore heresy because of her "male dress, claims to divine guidance, unorthodox behavior, and incredible success" (Solon 1982, 115). Alchemists worked hard, using scientific formulas, to find the elixir that would change lead into gold. As Michael Clanchy has said, "The borderline between science and magic—and reality and myth—was very fluid because each dealt in marvels and ancient esoteric knowledge." Further, he notes that "The distinction between magic and religion depended on the observer's point of view" (1997, 26). That "distinction between magic and religion" can still be difficult to discern. How many times have you knocked on wood, thrown salt over your shoulder, or avoided a black cat who seemed to want to cross your path? An anthropologist from another planet might scribble in her field notes, "Subject clings to primitive belief system."

Medieval people were not any more foolish or gullible than modern people can be. (Can you really lose thirty pounds in thirty days if you pay thirty dollars? Does the daily astrology column actually tell you how you should live? Is there seriously a monster living in Loch Ness?) They were ignorant, however, of some of the scientific principles, technology, and particularly medical knowledge that modern readers take for granted, such as how infectious diseases spread. They found other ways, sometimes ways that involved magic, to explain mysterious phenomena, phenomena that may seem simple to us. The mysterious and the supernatural were a part of daily existence. William Manchester captures one of the big differences between then and now in the title of his study of medieval society, *A World Lit Only by Fire* (1992). When no electric lights or even kerosene lanterns lit the corners of rooms on long winter nights, when firelight sent weird shadows racing across walls, when torchlight flickered and wavered in the outside air, things made much louder bumps in the night than they do when they can be expelled and explained with the flip of a light switch. Electric lights, along with changes in medical and scientific knowledge, have extinguished some of the mysteries medieval people lived with.

References to a belief in magic or the supernatural can be found within the most historically accurate novels. In *There Will Be Wolves*, Ursula stands trial for witchcraft, yet she knows she has done nothing out of the ordinary. In *The Witch's Brat* the villagers accuse Lovel of having the Evil Eye because his grandmother was a healer and because he is hunchbacked and has a twisted leg. Lovel himself believes he has healing powers which he refers to as the Old Skill. None of these beliefs held by the characters force us to categorize the novels as fantasy.

Interestingly, despite *Jackaroo* often being labeled fantasy, Voigt denies fantasy and the "old stories" more than any other of the writers discussed here by her insistence on realism. The old stories tell of a hero who takes from the rich to give to the poor. We call him Robin Hood; in the Kingdom, his name is Jackaroo. In the stories, he might have been the son of a king, or a fairy, but in Voigt's telling, no supernatural creatures help humans. Only humans help other humans. Voigt ennobles people by insisting that regular humans perform tasks that only supernatural folk can accomplish in other tales. How different is Gwyn, who finds ways to help her neighbors, and discovers how difficult it can be to help some people, from Dicey in Voigt's *Homecoming* (1981), who uses courage, invention, and persistence to find a home for herself and her siblings?

In *Jackaroo*, Gwyn learns how people see what they want or need to see. Jackaroo is as tall and as lordly as people need him to be, although Gwyn knows that in her own reality, Jackaroo is no more than a seventeen-year-old girl wearing leather boots, a scarlet cloak, and a plumed hat. But perhaps when she wears Jackaroo's clothing and performs Jackaroo's deeds she *is* tall and lordly? Reality is as one defines it.

According to Suzanne Rahn, when you "picture a knight in armor riding a black horse along a mountain road toward a distant castle . . . the story you imagine for him may be either historical fiction or fantasy" (1991, 1). Indeed, sometimes it's hard to tell the difference. So how can readers distinguish historical novels set in the European Middle Ages from fantasy novels? Try applying the following criteria, keeping in mind that a particular novel might not fit every element. Nor, or course, does the presence of one or two elements necessarily define the novel's genre.

Historical Novels Set in the Middle Ages

- The setting is a recognizable time period and place, although a particular village or town might be invented.
- Historical figures or events may be referred to.
- Christianity probably plays a role in characters' lives.
- Fantastic creatures (unicorns, dwarves, elves) are not characters, although the novel might refer to the belief in such creatures.
- Events do not happen because of magic, although characters might accept magic as real.
- The novel conforms to social and cultural aspects of the medieval period.

Fantasy Novels

- Supernatural or fantastic creatures may appear in the novel.
- Characters use magic to accomplish things.
- The setting, while it may be familiar-sounding, cannot be identified as an actual place.

Using these criteria, we can distinguish *The Hero and the Crown* and *Jackaroo* as fantasy, and *The Midwife's Apprentice* as historical fiction. But what of Katherine Paterson's retelling of a medieval romance in *Parzival: The Quest of the Grail Knight*? The medieval poem, like most medieval romances, is a fantasy, with its long-ago, far-away setting and its insistence on magic. Paterson's version, too, is fantasy, and the opening words define it as such: "In the ancient days, when Arthur was king of Britain" (1998, 3). There's an element of magic: The Grail is like a cornucopia—when a servant holds out a dish before it, the dish immediately overflows "with meats and fruits and rich foods of every kind" (52). Although Christianity plays a significant role in both the medieval and modern versions, the unspecified setting and the use of magic to accomplish things define them as fantasy, as do their representations of a social and cultural milieu. We see not aspects of a particular medieval period, but of a romanticized, fantasy landscape where shining knights ride out on quests and ladies recline in silk pavilions that are scattered throughout the forested wilderness. Just as reading Chaucer's *Nun's Priest's Tale*, where chickens suffer from love-longing and discuss dream theories, can tell us something about the Middle Ages without asking us to believe that what we are reading is realistic, readers can also learn about a time long past from *Parzival*. They discover that like us, medieval audiences enjoyed fantasies and legends and stories well told.

Well-told modern tales of the Middle Ages abound—thanks to novelists like Skurzynski and Cushman, Sutcliff and McGraw, Cadnum, Paterson, Alder, and Stolz. The writers who research carefully enough to understand the differences between medieval and modern attitudes, between different medieval settings, and between fantasy and history, can help their readers understand a strange and distant culture: the Middle Ages. Writers who create memorable, sympathetic characters who retain authentically medieval values teach their audience more than those who condescend to readers by sanitizing the past. Trusting readers to comprehend cultural differences, presenting the Middle Ages accurately, and telling a good story results in compelling historical fiction, fiction that, like medieval literature in its ideal form, teaches as it delights.

Welcome to Martin Library
Corinne checked out the following
items:

1. **Recasting the past : the
   Middle Ages in young
   adult literature**
   Barcode: 33454003469681
   Due: 11/18/2019

Today's Date: 10/28/2019 12:40
PM
You Saved $6.00 by borrowing
from the library!

Appendix

Into the Classroom

Classroom projects can enhance students' understanding of the medieval period as a culture distinct from our own. Instead of merely having students dress up as knights in armor and ladies in tall, pointed hats, with the result that they confuse Renaissance and medieval fashions (and thereby the Middle Ages with the Renaissance), it might be more instructive to let students research a particular moment in medieval history. Accessible reference works like *Daily Life in Chaucer's England* (1995) and Frances and Joseph Gies' series of books (see below) can add depth to students' understanding of medieval culture. Pairings of novels and medieval texts afford plenty of opportunities to explore traditional literary topics such as characterization and point of view, as well as writing strategies like comparison and dialogue.

Alun Hicks and Dave Martin (1997) describe a long-term project wherein students in English and history classes read the same historical novel. One of their assignments asks students to research a particular aspect of the Middle Ages and then to write a story based on that research. Working in groups on different research topics, students can query other groups for information that will help their own stories. This project, which could also be undertaken in an English class, gets students deeply involved in asking questions about the past and envisioning one aspect of life in a particular time period. It also makes them experts on specific topics who can then share their expertise with others.

Similarly, when a class reads a novel together, students themselves can determine whether or not the novel is historically accurate. After the class has listed the topics it needs more information about in order to make that determination, groups of students can research a single topic, such as apprenticeships or gender roles or rural life in a particular time period and place, before reporting to the class.

Below are more classroom activities and questions for discussion. The first set can be applied to any of the novels. These are supplemented by questions and activities for novels more likely to be used in the classroom, and followed by suggestions for further reading.

Questions and Activities

General Questions and Activities

- Write a short proposal for a novel, contemporary or historical, in which you will incorporate characters, plot elements, or events from a medieval text in the way Cadnum, Alder, or Temple do. You might base your entire novel on a medieval tale or event, or you might employ only snippets of information culled from your knowledge of the Middle Ages. Explain your rationale: How will your inclusion of these details enrich the text?

- Paterson chooses to retell an entire medieval poem in *Parzival: The Quest of the Grail Knight*. Rosemary Sutcliff does the same thing in her *Tristan and Iseult* and *Dragon Slayer: The Story of Beowulf*. If you were to retell a medieval poem or story for modern readers, which would you choose? Why? Would you look for literature with characters near your own age? What parts of the poem or story would you have to omit or explain? Try writing the opening paragraph and a paragraph (or a page) from the middle of your retelling. Or focus on a particular scene, such as Grendel approaching the hall where Beowulf awaits him.

- Choose a familiar story to retell (like Cinderella or Snow White or *Star Wars*). Use Cadnum's technique of employing or alluding to characters from *The Canterbury Tales* in your retelling. Explain why you would use a particular character of Chaucer's in each instance: for example, what details from Chaucer would help to characterize Cinderella's wicked stepmother? (Students need not have read *In a Dark Wood* to participate in this sort of activity.)

- Choose any of the novels and rewrite a short scene from the point of view of a different character in the same book. Consider the age, religion, gender, nationality, and social class of each character as you decide which details will be important. You may need to invent details that the first teller did not include.

- Look for places in historical novels where writers oversimplify in order to portray historical figures positively or negatively (as Alder does with Harold and William in *The King's Shadow*). Discuss ways the writer could show more complexity of characterization while still creating a character good or evil enough for the story.

- A surprising character narrates the story of *In a Dark Wood*: the villain of the Robin Hood stories, the Sheriff of Nottingham. Do you know of other novels told from the point of view of the villain? Plan your own retelling of a tale (medieval or modern) from the antagonist's point of view. How can you make your main character sympathetic? (Readers familiar with *Beowulf* and John Gardner's *Grendel* [1971] might look at the way Gardner allows the reader to sympathize with the monster.)

- Find a facsimile of the Luttrell Psalter. Compare the visual impression of one of the pictures with the descriptions of rural life in any of the novels. Which do you believe gives a more accurate vision of rural life in the late Middle Ages? Why? Write your own description of a medieval activity using a picture from The Luttrell Psalter as a guide. Or use pictures from the Bayeux Tapestry, where the focus is on the nobility during a time of war.

- Look at the way language, especially dialogue, is used in any of the novels. Does the writer use archaic diction or inverted word order to create a medieval flavor? Is it intrusive, taking the reader's attention away from the story, or does it add to the story? Keeping in mind that medieval people would not have sounded archaic or funny to each other, do you think using archaic language gives a good feeling for the Middle Ages? Look for places the writer uses interesting language for characterization, differentiating between the ways several characters, all of them medieval, speak. What other ways does the writer evoke a different time period? Compare archaic language in one of the novels to Chaucer's language, and then to Shakespeare's. Which seems closer to the language the novelist uses?

- Discuss ways in which writers do or do not create positive role models who have different moral sensibilities than we do. What other books do you know of (not necessarily set in the Middle Ages) in which characters accept societal views that we no longer accept? Is it all right for writers to change historical facts in order to teach readers about tolerance for diversity?

The Ramsay Scallop

Because *The Ramsay Scallop* is easily available in paperback and because of its awards (ALA Best Books for Young Adults, *Booklist* Editor's Choice "Top of the List"), it will probably end up being used in some classrooms despite its many historical inaccuracies. These inaccuracies can provide a gateway into a study of the Middle Ages. If students know that the novel is problematic but they don't know in what ways, they can be challenged to evaluate its portrayal of the medieval period themselves. The novel could easily be paired with *The Canterbury Tales* since it, too, revolves around a pilgrimage, and characters tell each other stories. Discussion might easily focus on the portrayal of medieval characters who have modern sensibilities and their reactions to *The Wife of Bath's Tale* and *The Clerk's Tale*.

- Compare Temple's characters' reactions to *The Clerk's Tale* with the reaction Chaucer's pilgrims have. In *The Canterbury Tales,* we hear the remarks of the Host and the Merchant. At the very end of the tale, the Host says he wishes his own wife could hear this story so that she would be more like Griselda. And at the beginning of his prologue, the Merchant compares his own wife's behavior—unfavorably—with Griselda's. How might Chaucer's Prioress and Wife of Bath have reacted? How would these reactions differ from those of Elenor or Marthe in *The Ramsay Scallop?* (Try this same exercise with *The Wife of Bath's Tale.*)

- Look at the story of Roland and the ensuing discussion of heroism in *The Ramsay Scallop* (169–75). How do you define the word *hero?* What qualities do your heroes possess? In your opinion, is Roland a hero? Keeping in mind that he is the hero of *The Song of Roland,* compare modern and medieval ideas of heroism.

- Turn the tables and have the medieval characters from *The Ramsay Scallop* tell a thoroughly modern story, such as the life and success of Bill Gates. How would Elenor and Thomas react to such a tale? How would real medieval teenagers react? How would their reactions differ from your own? Why?

- Discuss ways in which Temple could have revised her novel to make Elenor more characteristic of a thirteenth-century girl from rural England. Compare her to other protagonists you know who are from earlier time periods.

- Rewrite an episode from the novel that focuses on religion. See if you can give Elenor realistic reactions to Hassad or Pierre, for example.

Catherine, Called Birdy and *The Midwife's Apprentice*

- Discuss ways characters learn things in these two novels. What kinds of things that we would normally learn by reading about them do they learn in other ways? Compare the kinds of things you learn in ways other than reading about them. What kinds of things do you learn about better by doing than by reading about them? Compare our attitudes towards literacy with Birdy's or with Alyce's.

- Cushman weaves many details about medieval life into her novels. List some of the things you learned about daily life in the Middle Ages from reading one of her books (for example, how does Birdy kill fleas? What kinds of herbs does Jane Sharp use for what purposes? Do we still use any of the ones she uses?) Which details underscore the differences between rural England in 1290 and modern America? Which details show similarities between that world and ours?

- Were people more or less tolerant of diversity in 1290, when these novels were set, than they are now? What examples from the novels can you use to support your view?

- See if you can find the birth metaphors in *The Midwife's Apprentice* (for example, Alyce helping the cat out of the sack).

- Look at the language used by Edward, the little boy in *The Midwife's Apprentice*. Why does he use sentence constructions like, "I be leaving, mistress" or "I be going"? Does his language evoke an older time? How does it differ from Alyce's language? From Jane Sharp's?

The King's Shadow

- In *The King's Shadow*, Evyn reveres *The Song of Roland* and *Beowulf* because he wants to be a bard, or singer. He memorizes traditional, formulaic verses. If this story were updated to the present, what would Evyn want to be—a rock and roll star? A poet? What songs or poems would be appropriate for a modern Evyn to memorize? Why?

- In the novel, a storyteller recites verses from the end of *Beowulf*, recalling Beowulf's mortal battle with the dragon. Why do the characters in the novel think this story "is fitting for the heroes in this Hall" (207) when it tells of Beowulf's death in battle? Did it seem appropriate to you? Could Alder just as easily have used the story of Beowulf's fight with Grendel or with Grendel's mother here? Why or why not?

- Contrast the ideas of heroism presented within the novel through the excerpts from *Beowulf* and *The Song of Roland*. The Anglo-Saxons were known for their fatalism. How does their definition of a hero contrast with ours?

- Find a copy of the Anglo-Saxon poem, "The Battle of Maldon," in which the hero not only dies, but does so because (depending on the translation) of his own foolhardiness. Compare the ideas of heroism presented in "Maldon" to those throughout *The King's Shadow*.

- Find a copy of "The Battle of Brunanburh," part of which appears in the novel on pages 49–50. Discuss reasons you think Alder may have chosen these lines to include in the novel. What other lines might she also have chosen?

- Read and research *The Song of Roland*. Then compare the way the medieval poet oversimplifies heroes and villains to the way Alder treats William and Harold.

Further Reading

Novels

All of the following novels present, for the most part, historically accurate renderings of the medieval period.

Malcolm Bosse, *Captives of Time* (1987). This novel for older readers is set in late medieval Europe. After their parents are killed, two teenagers journey to the home of their uncle, who is developing a clock.

Bruce Clements, *Prison Window, Jerusalem Blue* (1977). Two Anglo-Saxon children are taken captive by Vikings.

Welwyn Wilton Katz, *Out of the Dark* (1996) is a contemporary novel with flashbacks to the eleventh-century Norse settlement in Newfoundland. Katz draws on *The Vinland Sagas,* Norse texts that record that settlement, in her skillful recreation of Viking life.

Cynthia Harnett, *The Cargo of the Madalena* (1959) is set in London in the 1480s, when Caxton has set up his printing press. Bendy's family are scribes, whose trade is in conflict with the new technology of book printing.

Mollie Hunter, *The King's Swift Rider* (1998). In fourteenth-century Scotland, Martin serves Robert the Bruce in his fight against the English.

E. L. Konigsburg, *A Proud Taste for Scarlet and Miniver* (1973) tells the story of Eleanor of Aquitaine and King Henry II from the point of view of Eleanor and her friends, who are in heaven.

Ellis Peters' Brother Cadfael mysteries, which take place in twelfth-century England, are generally historically accurate.

Ann Phillips, *The Peace Child* (1988). In fourteenth century England two babies are exchanged by their families to help stop a blood feud. One of them tells her story later, during a time of both the plague and the Peasants' Revolt of 1381.

Rosemary Sutcliff, *Sword Song* (1998). Published posthumously, this is the story of a ninth-century Viking teenager who lives as a warrior in Scotland.

Connie Willis, *Doomsday Book* (1992). Science fiction set in the mid-twenty-first century, this novel successfully captures fourteenth-century England during the plague years when the protagonist, an Oxford historian, time-travels there to conduct research.

General Works about the Middle Ages

Tania Bayard, *A Medieval Home Companion* (1991)

Anne Boyd, *Life in a Medieval Monastery* (1987)

Kevin Crossley-Holland, *The Anglo-Saxon World* (1982) (Translations of Anglo-Saxon poetry and prose)

Frances and Joseph Gies, *Life in a Medieval City* (1969), *Life in a Medieval Castle* (1974), *Women in the Middle Ages* (1978), *Marriage and Family in the Middle*

Ages (1987), *Life in a Medieval Village* (1990), and *A Medieval Family: The Pastons of Fifteenth-Century England* (1998)

Barbara Hanawalt, *Growing Up in Medieval London* (1993) and *The Middle Ages: An Illustrated History* (1998)

Urban Tigner Holmes, Jr., *Daily Living in the Twelfth Century* (1952)

Robert Lacey and Danny Danziger, *The Year 1000: What Life Was Like at the Turn of the First Millenium. An Englishman's World* (1999)

Norbert Ohler, *The Medieval Traveller* (1986)

Eileen Power, *Medieval People* (1924)

Shulamith Shahar, *Childhood in the Middle Ages* (1992)

Jeffrey Singman, *Daily Life in Medieval Europe* (1999)

Jeffrey Singman and Will McLean, *Daily Life in Chaucer's England* (1995)

Joseph R. Strayer, general editor, *The Dictionary of the Middle Ages* (1982)

Richard Vaughan's translation, *The Illustrated Chronicles of Matthew Paris: Observations on Thirteenth-Century Life* (1993)

Books About Manuscripts and Calligraphy

J.J.G. Alexander, *Medieval Illuminators and Their Methods of Work* (1992)

Michelle P. Brown, *Anglo-Saxon Manuscripts* (1991)

Michelle P. Brown and Patricia Lovett, *The Historical Source Book for Scribes* (1999)

Marc Drogin, *Medieval Calligraphy: Its History and Technique* (1980), *Anathema! Medieval Scribes and the History of Book Curses* (1983), *Yours Truly, King Arthur: How Medieval People Wrote, and How You Can, Too* (1983)

Christopher de Hamel, *A History of Illuminated Manuscripts* (1986) and *Scribes and Illuminators* (1992)

Bernard Meehan, *The Book of Kells* (1994)

Works Cited

Novels

Alder, E. 1995. *The King's Shadow*. New York: Farrar, Straus & Giroux.

Bosse, M. 1987. *Captives of Time*. New York: Bantam.

Bradford, K. 1992. *There Will Be Wolves*. New York: Dutton.

Cadnum, M. 1998. *In a Dark Wood*. New York: Orchard.

Clements, B. 1977. *Prison Window, Jerusalem Blue*. New York: Farrar, Straus & Giroux.

Cushman, K. 1994. *Catherine, Called Birdy*. New York: Clarion.

———. 1995. *The Midwife's Apprentice*. New York: Clarion.

Dana, B. 1991. *Young Joan*. New York: HarperCollins.

de Angeli, M. [1949] 1989. *The Door in the Wall*. New York: Bantam.

Furlong, M. 1995. *Robin's Country*. New York: Knopf.

Garden, N. 1995. *Dove and Sword: A Novel of Joan of Arc*. New York: Farrar, Straus & Giroux.

Gardner, J. 1971. *Grendel*. New York: Knopf.

Goodman, J.E. 1996. *The Winter Hare*. Boston: Houghton Mifflin.

Goodwin, M.D. 1989. *Where the Towers Pierce the Sky*. New York: Four Winds.

Gray, E.J. 1942. 1987. *Adam of the Road*. New York: Penguin.

Harnett, C. [1959] 1984. *The Cargo of the Madalena*. Minneapolis: Lerner.

Hunter, M. 1998. *The King's Swift Rider*. New York: HarperCollins.

Katz, W.W. 1996. *Out of the Dark*. New York: McElderry.

Kelly, E. [1928] 1961. *The Trumpeter of Krakow*. New York: Macmillan.

Konigsburg, E.L. 1973. *A Proud Taste for Scarlet and Miniver*. New York: Bantam.

McCaughrean, G. 1987. *A Little Lower than the Angels*. London: Puffin.

McGraw, E.J. 1991. *The Striped Ships*. New York: McElderry.

McKinley, R. 1984. *The Hero and the Crown*. New York: Greenwillow.

———. 1988. *The Outlaws of Sherwood*. New York: Greenwillow.

O'Dell, S. 1985. *The Road to Damietta*. Boston: Houghton Mifflin.

Paterson, K. 1988. *Park's Quest*. New York: Lodestar Books.

———. 1998. *Parzival: The Quest of the Grail Knight*. New York: Dutton.

Paulsen, G. 1993. *Nightjohn.* New York: Delacorte Press.

Phillips, Ann. 1988. *The Peace Child.* New York: Oxford University Press.

Pierce, T. 1983. *Alanna: The First Adventure.* New York: Atheneum.

———. 1986. *The Woman Who Rides Like a Man.* New York: Atheneum.

Skurzynski, G. [1979] 1993. *What Happened in Hamelin.* New York: Random.

———. 1999. *Spider's Voice.* New York: Atheneum.

Stolz, M. 1988. *Pangur Ban.* New York: HarperCollins.

Sutcliff, R. [1955] 1966. *The Shield Ring.* New York: Dell.

———. [1961] 1966. *Dragon Slayer: The Story of Beowulf.* New York: Penguin.

———. 1970. *The Witch's Brat.* New York: Walck.

———. 1971. *Tristan and Iseult.* New York: Dutton.

———. 1973. *Knight's Fee.* London: Oxford University Press.

———. 1998. *Sword Song.* New York: Farrar, Straus & Giroux.

Temple, F. 1994. *The Ramsay Scallop.* New York: Orchard Books.

Tolkien, J.R.R. 1937. *The Hobbit.* Boston: Houghton Mifflin.

Tomlinson, T. 1993. *The Forestwife.* New York: Orchard Books.

———. 1998. *Child of May.* New York: Orchard Books.

Trease, G. 1934. Rev. ed. 1966. *Bows Against the Barons.* London: Hodder and Stoughton.

Voigt, C. 1981. *Homecoming.* New York: Atheneum.

———. 1985. *Jackaroo.* New York: Atheneum.

Welch, R. [1954] 1979. *Knight Crusader.* New York: Oxford.

Willis, C. 1992. *Doomsday Book.* New York: Bantam.

Secondary Sources

Adamson, L.G. 1994. *Recreating the Past: A Guide to American and World Historical Fiction for Children and Young Adults.* Westport, CT: Greenwood.

Alexander, J.J.G. 1992. *Medieval Illuminators and Their Methods of Work.* New Haven and London: Yale University Press.

Archambault, P.J., trans. 1996. *A Monk's Confession: The Memoirs of Guibert of Nogent.* University Park: Pennsylvania State University Press.

Auerbach, E. [1946] 1957. *Mimesis.* Trans. W. Trask. New York: Doubleday Anchor Books.

Backhouse, J. 1990. *The Luttrell Psalter.* New York: New Amsterdam.

Barlow, F. 1970. *Edward the Confessor.* London: Eyre and Spottiswoode.

Bayard, T. 1991. *A Medieval Home Companion: Housekeeping in the Fourteenth Century.* New York: HarperCollins.

Bennett, J.A.W. and G.V. Smithers, eds. 1968. *Early Middle English Verse and Prose.* 2nd ed. Oxford: Oxford University Press.

Benson, L. ed. 1987. *The Riverside Chaucer.* 3rd ed. Boston: Houghton Mifflin.

Blamires, A. ed. 1992. *Woman Defamed and Woman Defended: An Anthology of Medieval Texts.* Oxford: Clarendon Press.

Boulton, D.J. 1998. "Earls and Earldoms." In *Medieval England: An Encyclopedia,* ed. P.E. Szarmach, M.T. Tavormina, and J.T. Rosenthal. New York: Garland.

Boyd, A. 1987. *Life in a Medieval Monastery.* Cambridge: Cambridge University Press.

Brewer, D. 1978. *Chaucer and His World.* Cambridge: D. S. Brewer.

Brown, G.H. 1998. "Alcuin." In *Medieval England: An Encyclopedia,* ed. P.E. Szarmach, M.T. Tavormina, and J.T. Rosenthal. New York: Garland.

———. 1995. "The Dynamics of Literacy in Anglo-Saxon England." *Bulletin of the John Rylands University Library of Manchester* 77: 109–42.

Brown, M.P. 1991. *Anglo-Saxon Manuscripts.* Toronto: University of Toronto Press.

Brown, M.P. and P. Lovett. 1999. *The Historical Source Book for Scribes.* Toronto: University of Toronto Press.

Campbell, J. ed. 1982. *The Anglo-Saxons.* London: Penguin.

Campbell, P. 1986. "The Young Adult Perplex." *Wilson Library Bulletin* 60.7 (March): 50–51.

Caxton, W. 1973. "From The Preface to the Aeneid." *The Oxford Anthology of English Literature.* Ed. F. Kermode and J. Hollander, 461–63. Vol. 1. New York: Oxford University Press.

Chibnall, M. 1984. *The World of Orderic Vitalis.* Rochester: Boydell.

Clanchy, M. T. 1993. *From Memory to Written Record: England 1066–1307.* 2nd ed. Oxford: Basil Blackwell.

———. 1997. *Abelard: A Medieval Life.* Oxford: Basil Blackwell.

Crawford, S.J., ed. [1922] 1969. *The Old English Version of the Heptateuch.* Early English Text Society original series 160. Reprint, with appendix, by N. R. Ker, London: Oxford University Press.

Cross, F.L. and E.A. Livingstone, eds. 1974. *The Oxford Dictionary of the Christian Church.* 2nd ed. Oxford: Oxford University Press.

de Hamel, C. 1986. *A History of Illuminated Manuscripts.* Boston: David R. Godine.

———. 1992. *Scribes and Illuminators.* Toronto: University of Toronto Press.

Drogin, M. 1980. *Medieval Calligraphy, Its History and Technique.* Montclair, NJ: Allanheld and Schram.

———. 1983. *Anathema! Medieval Scribes and the History of Book Curses.* Montclair, NJ: Allanheld and Schram.

———. 1983. *Yours Truly, King Arthur: How Medieval People Wrote, and How You Can, Too.* New York: Taplinger Publishing Company.

Fleming, R. 1998. "Domesday Book." In *Medieval England: An Encyclopedia,* ed. P.E. Szarmach, M.T. Tavormina, and J.T. Rosenthal. New York: Garland.

Frank, R.W. 1986. "The Canterbury Tales III: Pathos." In *The Cambridge Chaucer Companion,* ed. P. Boitani and J. Mann, 143–158. Cambridge: Cambridge University Press.

Garrison, J. 1996. "A Transactional Reading of Cynthia Voigt's *Jackaroo.*" *The ALAN Review* 23: 12–21.

Gies, F. and J. 1969. *Life in a Medieval City.* New York: Crowell.

———. 1974. *Life in a Medieval Castle.* New York: HarperCollins.

———. 1978. *Women in the Middle Ages.* New York: Crowell.

———. 1987. *Marriage and Family in the Middle Ages.* New York: Harper and Row.

———. 1990. *Life in a Medieval Village.* New York: HarperCollins.

———. 1994. *Cathedral, Forge, Waterwheel: Technology and Invention in the Middle Ages.* New York: HarperCollins.

———. 1999. *A Medieval Family: The Pastons of Fifteenth-Century England.* New York: HarperCollins.

Hanawalt, B.A. 1993. *Growing Up in Medieval London.* New York: Oxford University Press.

———. 1998. *The Middle Ages: An Illustrated History.* New York: Oxford University Press.

Herz, S.K. and D.R. Gallo. 1996. *From Hinton to Hamlet: Building Bridges Between Young Adult Literature and the Classics.* Westport, CT: Greenwood.

Heslop, T.A. 1992. "Eadwine and his Portrait." In *The Eadwine Psalter,* ed. M. Gibson, R.A. Heslop, and R.W. Pfaff. London and University Park: The Modern Humanities Research Association and The Pennsylvania State University Press: 178–85.

Hicks, A. and D. Martin. 1997. "Teaching English and History Through Historical Fiction." *Children's Literature in Education* 28: 49–59.

Holmes, U.T. 1952. *Daily Living in the Twelfth Century.* Madison: University of Wisconsin Press.

Isaac, M.L. 2000. *Heirs to Shakespeare: Reinventing the Bard in Young Adult Literature.* Portsmouth, NH: Heinemann/Boynton Cook.

Katzenstein, R. 1991. "Medieval and Renaissance Manuscripts of the Bible: An Introduction to the Exhibition at the J. Paul Getty Museum." *A Thousand Years of the Bible: An Exhibition of Manuscripts from the J. Paul Getty Museum.* Malibu and Los Angeles: The J. Paul Getty Museum and the University of California Press.

Keenan, C. 1997. "Reflecting a New Confidence: Irish Historical Fiction for Children." *The Lion and the Unicorn* 21: 369–78.

Ker, N.R. 1957. *Catalogue of Manuscripts Containing Anglo-Saxon.* Oxford: Clarendon.

Keynes, S. and M. Lapidge, eds. 1983. *Alfred the Great: Asser's Life of King Alfred and Other Contemporary Sources*. Harmondsworth: Penguin.

Kittredge, G.L. 1911–12. "Chaucer's Discussion of Marriage." *Modern Philology* 9: 435–67.

Knowles, D. 1962. *The Evolution of Medieval Thought*. New York: Vintage.

Lacey, R. and D. Danziger. 1999. *The Year 1000. What Life Was Like at the Turn of the First Millenium: An Englishman's World*. Boston: Little, Brown.

Ladurie, E.L. [1975] 1979. *Montaillou: The Promised Land of Error*. Trans. B. Bray. New York: Vintage.

Lefferts, P.M. and R. Rastall. 1998. "Minstrels and Minstrelsy." In *Medieval England: An Encyclopedia*, ed. P.E. Szarmach, M.T. Tavormina, and J.T. Rosenthal. New York: Garland.

Little, L.K. 1982. "Francis of Assisi, St." In *The Dictionary of the Middle Ages*, ed J.R. Strayer. New York: Charles Scribner's Sons.

MacLeod, A.S. 1998. "Writing Backwards: Modern Models in Historical Fiction." *Horn Book* 74 (Jan/Feb): 26–33.

MacRae, C.D. 1998. *Presenting Young Adult Fantasy Fiction*. New York: Twayne.

Manchester, W. 1992. *A World Lit Only by Fire*. Boston: Little, Brown.

Margolis, S. 1996. "Breathing Life into the Middle Ages for Young Adults." *School Library Journal* 42: 36–7.

McNulty, J.B. 1998. "Bayeux Tapestry." In *Medieval England: An Encyclopedia*, ed. P.E. Szarmach, M.T. Tavormina, and J.T. Rosenthal. New York: Garland.

Meehan, B. 1994. *The Book of Kells*. London: Thames and Hudson.

Miller, M.Y. 1994. "'The Rhythm of a Tongue': Literary Dialect in Rosemary Sutcliff's Novels of the Middle Ages for Children." *Children's Literature Association Quarterly* 19: 25–31.

———. 1995. "'Thy Speech is Strange and Uncouth': Language in the Children's Historical Novel of the Middle Ages." *Children's Literature* 23: 71–90.

Ohler, N. [1986] 1989. *The Medieval Traveller*. Trans. C. Hillier. Woodbridge, England: Boydell.

Pelteret, D.A. 1995. *Slavery in Early Medieval England*. Woodbridge, England: Boydell.

Pernoud, R. [1962] 1994. *Joan of Arc: By Herself and Her Witnesses*. Trans. E. Hyams. Lanham, MD: Scarborough House.

Power, E. [1924] 1963. *Medieval People*. New York: HarperCollins.

Radice, B. 1974. *The Letters of Abelard and Heloise*. London: Penguin.

Rahn, S. 1991. "An Evolving Past: The Story of Historical Fiction and Nonfiction for Children." *The Lion and the Unicorn* 15: 1–26.

Reid, S.E. 1995. *Presenting Cynthia Voigt*. New York: Twayne.

Review of *Jackaroo*, by Cynthia Voigt. 1985. *Bulletin for the Center for Children's Books* 39.1 (September): 19.

Rowling, M. 1968. *Life in Medieval Times*. New York: Perigee Books.

Saenger, P. 1982. "Silent Reading: Its Impact on Late Medieval Script and Society." *Viator* 13: 367–414.

Sancha, S. 1982. *The Luttrell Village: Country Life in the Middle Ages*. New York: Crowell.

Shahar, S. 1983. *The Fourth Estate: A History of Women in the Middle Ages*. Trans. C. Galai. London: Routledge.

———. 1990. *Childhood in the Middle Ages*. Trans. C. Galai. London: Routledge.

Singman, J.L. 1999. *Daily Life in Medieval Europe*. Westport, CT: Greenwood.

———. and W. McLean. 1995. *Daily Life in Chaucer's England*. Westport, CT: Greenwood.

Smith, A.H. 1966. *The Parker Chronicle 832–900*. New York: Appleton-Century-Crofts.

Smith, K. 1985. Review of *Jackaroo* by Cynthia Voigt. *School Library Journal* 32 (December): 96.

Solon, P. 1982. "Joan of Arc, St." In *The Dictionary of the Middle Ages*, ed J.R. Strayer. New York: Charles Scribner's Sons.

Southern, R.W., ed. 1972. *The Life of St. Anselm, Archbishop of Canterbury, by Eadmer*. Oxford: Clarendon Press.

Stanford, A. 1985. "A Link with the Past: Ninth-century Manuscripts Discovered in Rare Book Collection." *Endeavors: Research and Graduate Education at The University of North Carolina at Chapel Hill* 2.2: 8–9.

Strayer, J.R., gen. ed. 1982. *Dictionary of the Middle Ages* 13 vols. New York: Charles Scribner's Sons.

Sullivan, C.W. 1992. "Real-izing the Unreal: Folklore in Young Adult Science Fiction and Fantasy." In *Literature for Children: Contemporary Criticism*, ed. P. Hunt, 140–55. London, Routledge.

Vaughan, R., trans. 1993. *The Illustrated Chronicles of Matthew Paris*. Dover, NH: Alan Sutton Publishing.

von Eschenbach, W. 1961. *Parzival*. Trans. H.M. Mustard and C.E. Passage. New York: Vintage.

Ward, B. 1987. *Miracles and the Medieval Mind*. Philadelphia: University of Pennsylvania Press.

Whitelock, D. 1961. *The Anglo-Saxon Chronicle*. New Brunswick: Rutgers University Press.

Wilson, D. 1985. *The Bayeux Tapestry*. New York: Knopf.

Young, C.R. 1998. "Forests, Royal." In *Medieval England: An Encyclopedia*, ed. P.E. Szarmach, M.T. Tavormina, and J.T. Rosenthal. New York: Garland.

Index